HOW TO GET INTO RADIO

In this Series

Other titles in preparation

GET INTO RADIO

Starting your career as a radio broadcaster

Bernie Simmons

How To Books

British Library Cataloguing-in-Publication data
A catalogue record for this book is available from the British Library.

© Copyright 1995 by Bernie Simmons

First published in 1995 by How To Books Ltd, Plymbridge House, Estover Road, Plymouth PL6 7PZ, United Kingdom.
Tel: Plymouth (01752) 735251/695745. Fax: (01752) 695699.
Telex: 45635.

Note: The material contained in this book is set out in good faith for general guidance and no liability can be accepted for loss or expense incurred as a result of relying in particular circumstances on statements made in the book. The laws and regulations are complex and liable to change, and readers should check the current position with the relevant authorities before making personal arrangements.

Typeset by Kestrel Data, Exeter.
Printed and bound in Great Britain by The Cromwell Press, Broughton Gifford, Melksham, Wiltshire.

Contents

List of Illustrations

Preface

It is the aim of this book to prepare you, as a would-be radio broadcaster, with enough knowledge and know-how to make a good start on your career.

I can personally testify to a broadcaster's humble beginnings as a pub and club jock. The thrills (and spills) of helping the 5-star hotel champagne set rock the night away, overseas as well as in Park Lane. And the enlightening 'apprenticeship', as a 16-year-old on West Middlesex Hospital Radio in 1979, in-store Radio Top Shop in Northern England and Radio HMV, Oxford Street, W1. Then the most exciting opportunities in real radio began to unfold, and continue to do so. I have subsequently presented a diversity of programmes ranging from overnights, mid-mornings and breakfast on Independent Local Radio, including 'Hot Hits' Top 40 radio like Power FM, the nostalgic County Sound Gold and news magazine and phone-in programmes on Community Radio, to freelancing for the most highly respected world-wide radio services: the BBC World Service, and BFBS Radio. Along the way I have voiced countless radio and television commercials, promotional films and narrations, as well as having been previously published as a celebrity feature writer in the pop music and TV press in Britain, the USA, Australia and Germany.

I hope that *How to Get Into Radio* also serves to inspire in you a passion for radio, and encourages the confidence and self-determination that you will need to develop a successful career as a broadcaster.

I would also like to extend my warmest gratitude to all those kind people, friends and colleagues who went out of their way to help me with research information and materials. Josephine, thank you for your undying love and support, and Ernest, toast never tasted better than with large dollops of your very delicious home-made strawberry jam!

Bernie Simmons

Is this you?

Good voice

Positive outlook

Friendly

Quick learner

Interested in people

Adaptable

Sociable

Tolerant

Good personality

Well organised

Lots of interests

Courteous

Practical

Reliable

Alert

Responsible

Punctual

Mature attitude

Outgoing

Ready for a challenge

Calm in a crisis

Confident

Articulate

Team worker

Active

Good planner

Self-disciplined

Willing to help

Listener

Prepared to travel

Respectful of others

Good coper

Good host

Good general knowledge

Open-minded

1
Understanding Radio

HOW DID IT ALL BEGIN?

The world's first radio station went on the air in America. That is, the first station with a complete programme schedule and regular complement of talking bow-ties and Gatsby shoes was *Station KDKA*, Pittsburgh in 1920. Dubious claims to 'radio firsts' are made by other countries: to this day, the Russians observe May 7th as Radio Day, because the radio pioneer Alexander Popov performed a radio demonstration on May 7th 1895. The Dutch and the Canadians also claim to have begun regular radio services in 1919.

The new 'wireless' technology of the day was arousing so much interest and excitement that in America the government (in true spirit-of-free-enterprise fashion) didn't initially see the need to regulate or control the spread of radio stations across the states. By the end of 1921 there were 30 stations in America, and by the end of 1927 there were 1,000.

When did radio start in Britain?

Commercial radio in America flourished from the word 'go', and there was certainly enough interest from the radio set manufacturers to start broadcasting their own commercial services in Britain. A few large firms in Britain were given experimental licences to broadcast in the early 1920s. The wireless pioneer Guglielmo Marconi transmitted historical broadcasts from stations in London and Chelmsford using the code name 2LO.

The British government of the day were carefully watching the early exploits of American radio and came to the conclusion that advertisements on the radio were 'vulgar and intrusive'. So, in Britain commercial radio was well and truly filibustered. The postmaster general, who was given the responsibility of suggesting ways in which the public could best benefit from this new invention, decided that instead of letting commercial operators broadcast freely, '. . . a public corporation (the BBC) be set up . . . acting as trustee for the national interest . . .' In other words, the government thought radio to be so powerful a mass media tool that they could not leave the responsibility for its influence in the hands of commercial operators. At the highest level, paranoia prevailed concerning its wrongful applications, like propaganda.

IS RADIO ALL THAT POWERFUL?

Radio certainly has the power to stir an entire nation into panic. A case in point was the now infamous, perhaps irresponsible, Orson Welles broadcast on 30th October 1938 on the Columbia Broadcasting System (CBS) of a radio dramatisation of HG Wells' *War of the Worlds*. Millions of Americans at home with their families heard what appeared to be live, on-the-spot reportage of Martians invading New Jersey, New York, at peak listening time on Hallowe'en Night. The station was broadcasting a scheduled classical music programme which was suddenly interrupted with a dramatised news-flash describing the terrors of a Martian invasion, before returning to the music programme. In a second dramatised news-flash, an actor playing the part of the then president Roosevelt was heard to address the nation and announce a state of emergency. Not surprisingly it caused mass panic across America.

Thousands of petrified listeners jammed the station's phone lines and even the confused New York police were sent to the CBS studios and stood in the control room watching the drama being acted out, not sure whether they were dealing with a real emergency or whether they should be arresting anyone. If the broadcast proved anything, it asserted the power of radio to be able to communicate a message to an entire nation. The perpetrator of the 'prank', Orson Welles, intended to prove the point that people 'would believe it [*ie* anything] if they heard it on the radio'.

World leaders such as Winston Churchill during the world war of 1939–45, and President Roosevelt during the American depression of the 1930s respectively were able to deliver important updates to an entire nation through the medium of radio. Queen Elizabeth II has addressed the Commonwealth, and the Pope has reached the world, through radio. In most recent times, radio has been used to great effect, and during the conflicts in Haiti, Bosnia, Rwanda and South Africa radio broadcasts proved an indispensable way of keeping people informed.

HOW DID THE BBC START?

The BBC was born on 1st January 1927. Formerly the **British Broadcasting Company**, made up by a consortium of six of the leading manufacturers of the first 'wireless' radio sets (like General Electric—later GEC, and PYE), it became the **British Broadcasting Corporation**. Almost immediately, a licence fee was introduced for the right to receive its programmes, payable on purchase of the wireless set. The BBC has become the most respected broadcasting organisation worldwide for its accuracy and integrity of reporting and quality of programming. However, creating the BBC to take full control or rather, 'maternal responsibility' (the BBC soon after became affectionately known as 'Auntie') for radio, right from the start, was to see to it that Britain would have to wait nearly *50 years* for commercial radio to flourish freely.

The first two independent stations arrived in the shape of LBC (London Broadcasting Company) Radio on 6th October 1973 and Capital Radio ten days later.

HOW IS RADIO IN BRITAIN STRUCTURED TODAY?

In Britain, radio is divided into four main groups:

1. BBC radio
BBC World Service

National network radio
Radio 1, Radio 2, Radio 3, Radio 4 and Radio 5 Live.

National regional radio
BBC Scotland (comprising 4 local stations), BBC Northern Ireland (comprising 2 local stations) and BBC Wales (comprising 3 local stations).

BBC local radio
Comprises around 40 individual stations whose typical coverage is English counties such as BBC Southern Counties Radio, for Surrey and Sussex, plus stations dedicated to large metropolitan areas, such as BBC Greater Manchester Radio (GMR).

2. Independent national radio (INR)
There are now three national commercial radio services for Britain:

Fig. 1. ILR radio map of the UK.

Classic FM: classical music
Talk Radio UK: speech-based news and talkback
Virgin 1215: rock and pop music

3. Independent local radio (ILR)

Independent commercial radio relies on advertising and sponsorship
(a typical example of a sponsored message on commercial radio: '. . .
this travel update is brought to you by NEC mobile phones . . .').
They are its only source of revenue; unlike BBC radio which receives
95% of its funding from the TV licence and government grants, and
the other five per cent from commercial enterprise. BBC World
Service radio is funded solely by the Foreign Office.

There are around 160 commercial stations comprising ILR, community and five new 'regional' stations in Britain, broadcasting a wide
variety of services on AM and FM. (See ILR Radio Map of the UK,
fig 1.)

4. Satellite and cable radio

A number of services broadcast a type of popular radio referred to as
'satellite radio' or 'cable radio'. Although these services simply
resemble radio in their style, they broadcast on satellite TV and cable
TV channels. Other stations have discovered the additional scope
of a Europe-wide coverage by broadcasting their services via the
spare audio channels of cable and satellite TV stations; among
them Radio 1 and Virgin 1215, which can be listened to in stereo on
satellite.

1000s OF NEW JOBS

During 1996 the Radio Authority will make available a section of the
FM spectrum that has never before been allocated to stations in
Britain.

Until now, the space available for permanent stations to broadcast
has been 87.5 MHz (on the left of the FM dial) to 105 MHz (on the
right). The FM dial has in reality always stretched as far as 108 MHz;
and it is this extra space which will accommodate up to 90 additional
permanent services. Most of these new services will be low-powered
community radio stations . . . and they will all need to be staffed (see
Chapter 10).

Added to this, another transmission development is going to
revolutionise the way the world listens to and operates radio for ever:

Digital Audio Broadcasting (DAB)

The new **digital** radio services of the future will be found on the higher reaches of the frequency spectrum. The benefits of improved reception and sound quality will be on a par with the difference between the crackly old (analogue) LP and the much improved CD. At the risk of confusing you if you're not technically minded, it simply means that the new technology will allow up to six new services to be crammed into the space of 1.5 MHz on the FM dial.

So, with all this expansion coming, what a glorious time it is to be thinking about a career in radio!

IS THE RADIO BUSINESS AS LUCRATIVE AS TV?

Those personalities earning big wages in radio are the exception; they are probably TV celebrities who also happen to make regular appearances on the radio.

Radio isn't as lucrative as TV. It's far more expensive to make a television programme, because the processes and technology are more complex and expensive. Most television programmes require the contribution of a whole crew of specialists, all of whose wages have to be paid, pushing up the cost of making the programme. So, to recover the costs of buying the programmes to show, television stations have to charge very high advertising rates.

Shoestring budgeting

In contrast, radio programmes can be made on a shoestring budget. Radio can be a one-person operation. The research, production, technical operating and performance of a radio programme can very conceivably all be delivered by one-and-the-same person. On a good many small local radio outfits with tighter spending budgets, pro-grammes are indeed a one-person operation. This is why local or community radio is a good place to cut your broadcasting teeth as you'll have the opportunity to get involved and experience the various stages in the programme making and broadcasting process. So, whilst radio can claim to be the grandfather of broadcasting, it would be wrong to deny that it has become the poor relation to television—and it's all down to money.

It's a fact that, in Britain, radio is not yet as attractive an advertising medium as TV. The same is not true of the United States, where radio gives TV a good run for its money—literally.

So, is it possible to make a good living from radio?

To further identify the 'colour' of radio, we will again place it next to the 'colour' of TV, its nearest relative. TV personalities who deliver good viewing ratings become indispensable and are invited back again and again to front yet another new series. They eventually demand ridiculous fees.

Fortune could smile on you, too, as radio stations become more ratings conscious. If you can deliver good listening figures, the station won't want to let go of a good thing. But, the gulf between a high earning radio personality and TV personality is still immense.

Typical salaries for staff and freelance broadcasters range from £12–25,000. And your chances of becoming a 'local celebrity' are fairly good but you won't get rich working on radio. In fact it's not uncommon for some of the smaller local and community stations to start novice broadcasters on fees of £25 or £30 per radio programme presented.

You can build a satisfying career and achieve an above average standard of living if you're good. There are opportunities to use the experience you've gained as a broadcaster to springboard into other areas and increase your earning power, such as voice-overs, feature writing and TV continuity announcing and even TV presenting.

Job security is very difficult to gauge, especially for the freelance (see Chapter 3).

WHAT TYPES OF PEOPLE WORK IN RADIO?

All sorts. Some highly educated and some without any formal qualifications at all. Good-looking people and ugly people. You'll work with intellectual egg-heads and alongside natural clowns who're always laughing at the world. You'll meet the oldies who've '. . . been in broadcasting for more than 40 years, laddie . . .' and glassy-eyed 16-year-old slaves, ecstatic at the chance to run-and-fetch for everybody and get paid a pittance.

People come to radio from many different walks of life, backgrounds, religious and sexual orientation. But having said that, there are certain 'personality traits' that are common among all broadcasters, and you should be able to recognise yourself in most of the following:

- you're a good conversationalist
- you're able to relate to all sorts of people
- you're curious . . . *'why?'* is your favourite word

- you have a sense of responsibility for people
- you're very opinionated and know what's best
- you love a bit of gossip
- you're analytical
- you like working with people
- you're outwardly an extrovert but really a loner
- you're quick-witted
- you're the restless and nervy type.

SUMMING UP

In this opening chapter, you have journeyed right back to the very beginning of 'wireless radio broadcasting'. You've learned the name of the very first 'fully scheduled' radio station, Station KDKA, Pittsburgh, and how quickly radio spread in the United States as early as the 1920s. And HOW and WHY and WHEN the world famous British Broadcasting Corporation came about. All vital knowledge for the future broadcaster—as they say, 'how can you know where you're going, if you don't know where you're coming from?'

We rounded off this opening chapter by bringing you bang up to date. Laying out the structure of today's exciting radio networks. And the reasons why job opportunities will boon be opening up for you. The radio map on page 15 perfectly illustrates how swiftly this era of expansion is unfolding before us. Pretty soon there won't be space to fit them all in!

2
A Day in the Life of . . .
a Radio Show Host

THE DAY STARTS HERE!

06.00 wakes up to the sounds of the breakfast show.

06.30 has breakfast and reads the papers.

08.00 arrives at the station.

08.05 sorts through pigeon-hole for memos, messages and picks up
the programme print-out.

08.10 grabs another coffee and reads the mail.

08.20 prepares a list of songs for music librarian to find.

08.30 sits down with programme assistant to discuss the day's
programme features, interviews and competitions.

09.00 goes into a spare production studio to pre-record the clues to
instant phone-in competition.

09.15 rewrites some gossip and silly news items from the papers.

09.25 attempts to find appropriate newspaper stories to fit in with
the music choices on the running order.

09.35 grabs another coffee.

09.45 adrenalin starts pumping—15 minutes to air!

09.50 major news story breaks—the Spanish have invaded Gibraltar.
Head of news asks for two extra news updates an hour until

Fig. 2. An 'on-air' broadcast desk.

Fig. 3. A CD cart player.

further notice. Throwing running order into chaos. It means dropping items. Which ones?

09.55 the guest interviewee calls to say she will be arriving an hour late, sending running order into further chaos.

09.58 goes into studio. Cues up personal ID jingles and first song, mimes the weather report and times it silently.

09.59 head of news calls to say ten o'clock bulletin will be extended to around 12 minutes.

10.01 hot-seat change with preceding presenter during the news: plenty of time to re-organise running order.

10.12 the red light flashes 'on-air' above the door outside. 'Good morning. Well, what a day it's been already and we haven't even started yet; we will of course keep you updated with any further developments on . . . so stay with us'.

SHADOWING A PRO: SITTING IN ON A LIVE SHOW

And now you're sitting in the studio watching the professional at work . . . the next CD to be played is being put into a funny-looking plastic case . . .

'Why are you putting the CD into a plastic case?'
'All the music played on radio these days is played on high audio quality CD. We play CDs on professional cartridge machines; by putting the CD into a case you create the cartridge to put in the machine (*see Fig 3.*). The reason for doing it this way is to allow faster access to individual tracks. You just turn a dial to the track number you want and cue the song on the disc instantly.

'The CD machine also gives us a more accurate duration reading; it can count up from the beginning of a song or backwards from the total, which lets you know how long the song has to run.

'We usually have three such machines at any one time, in case one CD plays up or skips there is another one all ready to play. You also play jingles and strange sound effects on CD. You have the opportunity to be really creative, but for that you need more than one machine.'

The headphones that were resting on the mixing desk are slipped on again. Arms spread-eagle over the mixing desk (fig 2 shows an on-air studio mixing desk); the left hand is holding one of the faders, the fingers of the right hand are poised over a red-lit button. The song is fading out, the left hand pulls open the microphone fader, cutting-out the studio speakers, and we're live again.

'. . . London City 107 FM plays the kind of music that makes you feel human again. That's what I live for; coming into this studio day after day and playing music that I know is going to do you good. Incidentally, if life isn't treating you very well at the moment, I want to know about it—find the time to drop me a line anytime . . .'

With that, the red-lit button is squeezed gently and the next CD starts to play. The microphone is cut out and the headphones come off again.

'You have lots of people listening, yet you seem to be talking to one person. Why's that?'
'Most people listen to the radio on their own. One of the easiest ways of telling a novice broadcaster from a pro is that a novice will shout at the listener and say things like, "Hello *everyone!*" It's quite understandable and forgivable. To a new broadcaster suddenly given the task of broadcasting to an entire county, say, comprising a regular audience running into tens of thousands, it might seem the right thing to address them as a crowd. But this is wrong because for the most part radio is a one-to-one communication medium—best demonstrated by what is known as *public access radio:* the phone-in. The total sum of the listeners is *not* all packed into a stadium and listening in a mass crowd. Suppose, as is the case with most radio listeners, you're listening on your own, isn't it more pertinent if the voice addressed you, and you alone.

'As you gain experience and make contact with your listeners via letters and phone calls and outside broadcasts you will come to realise who is out there "on the other side of the microphone"—prepare for a few surprises . . . nice and not so nice (ranging from the harmless weirdo to the mentally unbalanced); all life is out there in radio land.

'One thing to be very conscious of, if you work on a commercial station, is getting your ad breaks out on time.'

'Does the presenter have the responsibility for playing the adverts?'
'On some programmes, you have an assistant or producer to take care of this for you, though you can also be on your own. But, in most cases the presenter has to make sure they're played, and most crucially, played on time. You have to be aware that advertisers have opted to pay a certain rate to have their commercial played in certain

prime slots in the day or the programme. Adverts are the life-blood for a commercial station; it relies on advertising revenue for its survival. You can imagine the fuss if a commercial was played later than promised, or missed out all together! In fact, playing the ads is very easy now. All you have to do is press this "GO" button and the entire ad break, which might have three or four different ads loaded together, will be played in sequence by the computer. All you really need to be aware of is the duration in minutes of the break, and to watch for the end, so you can slip in a station identification jingle before playing the next CD.

'How do the jingles get played?'
'Until the advent of computers in radio studios, we used to record each jingle, and commercial for that matter, on an individual, 30, 40 or 50 second cart. It is basically a tape cartridge in which the tape has been arranged in a kind of loop. It plays at the touch of a button, automatically fast-forwards itself, and is always ready to play. That's very useful when you need to play something quickly in a live situation.

'Traditionally, an entire wall of carts would adorn one of the studio walls, or there would be a large carousel next to the mixing desk. It would contain individual presenter name checks, station jingles and commercials. Just as records and turntables are being phased out, so too are carts as more and more of what is played is recorded digitally and played in remotely or by a computer touch screen by the presenter.'

(*A few* **segues** *are in order; it seems you have a lot of questions on your mind. The broadcaster* **back-annos** *the song,* **points** *to a new competition starting next week and announces three-in-a-row.*) Puzzled by any jargon? See the Glossary on page 127.

'Why do people listen to the radio?'
'Many thousands of hours of market research have been spent on that question. Radio is certainly the big ratings winner in the mornings with an audience *two and half times* the size of all commercial television and *11 times* the size of 'The Big Breakfast' on Channel 4 at the crucial 8am point.'

'The overwhelming reason for radio's popularity is simply that people can be entertained and informed by the radio while doing something else, like the housework, at the same time without missing anything. Radio beats TV hands down in this respect and this point may go a long way to explain why radio wasn't driven to extinction as people had predicted. This, and the fact that we all love to exercise our imagination, given the opportunity. By its very nature, radio forces the listener to imagine the scenarios and the stories being described. It's fun trying to put a face to a voice too—and, incidentally, you'll discover that 99% of the time no broadcaster actually looks the way s/he sounds. Television usually requires your full attention. Once you're in front of the box, you're immobilised; you can't do something else or you'll miss half of it.

'When it comes to radio listening, it doesn't take any effort at all to drive a car and listen; do the housework and listen; have a bath and listen; do the cooking and listen; write a book . . . and listen. Other more significant research into radio listening has revealed that generally people use the radio as their most immediate news and weather source (satellite-delivered TV news services like CNN and Sky News notwithstanding), followed statistically by the need for accurate time checks.

'People also listen to the radio for company, and to many thousands of lonely, depressed or elderly people, the person who "comes back on the radio" like magic at the same time every day can become their best friend. A very real person on tap, reliably on time, being funny or talking about something interesting.'

For no apparent reason, three lines on the studio switchboard suddenly start to blink excitedly.

'Ah, there they go, my darlings want to get involved . . . I wonder what they want?' *He starts to answer them one by one, and is hurriedly scribbling people's birthdays and place names on the back of a press release.*

'That was an interesting one; it's a guy who's too shy to ask his girlfriend to marry him, so he wants me to do it for him—on the air! Somebody once phoned me to say her car had been stolen. The thing that annoyed me was the fact that it happened in a hospital car park; she'd been visiting her sick mother. So, I told the story on-air with a description of the car and the story obviously sickened a few listeners. Within an hour the police phoned me to say that listeners had reported sightings, and they found the car. The robbers had probably been listening to my programme too and quickly abandoned it.'

'Who listens to the radio?'
'You can have a good idea of what your listeners are going to be like, but you'll never get to know them all. The majority will never have the slightest desire to make themselves known to you. On a general entertainment station, a typical local BBC or ILR station, the demographic or age-range of the listeners could well mean that your regular listeners will range from kiddies aged six or seven, to wise old

folk gracefully seeing out the evening of their lives in a retirement haven.'

'What are listeners doing while they're listening?'
'That's anybody's guess. If they're really lucky, they'll be tucked up with their favourite person, with you blabbering on in the background. Some will be washing their hair, pruning the roses, sitting on a bus, sunning themselves in the park or working belly-side up under a car. It's important to be conscious of the fact that your listeners will be getting up to all manner of activities and not necessarily waiting for you to try to get them to indulge in an inappropriate activity like dancing, for example.

'There have been humorous cases involving less astute club and disco DJs who cross over to radio and whose only experience has been to create a party atmosphere and cajole people into "getting down on it man!" in horrendously imitated mid-Atlantic accents. You have to consider your audience very carefully.'

Someone is pressing their face up against the little window in the studio door, and pulling a funny face.

'That's Shirley, the receptionist . . . probably to tell me that my guest has arrived.' *He waves her into the studio.*

'Hello, darling, Lisa Stansfield's arrived. When do you want her?'

'She's early . . . er . . . not for another half an hour. Would you get her a coffee or something, and I'll come out and say hello in a minute.'

'Are interviews easy to handle?'
'That all depends on how well prepared you are. Unless you know the person you're talking to intimately, you will have to read up on them; press releases, recent magazine features and so on. It would be embarrassing to get your facts wrong. Usually, the person being interviewed is getting more out of being there than you are. They might want to promote a new book, album, film or event, so it's a wonderful opportunity to get some free publicity. At the same time the station (and the programme) benefits from an added attraction for the listeners.

'From a practical viewpoint it's very important that you remain in control of the interview at all times. You will want to steer the conversation in such a way as suits you and fits into your programme. That said, you don't have to stick to your questions so rigidly as to sound mechanical; *listen* to the person, give them space to think and speak, and try not to butt in and spoil the flow.

'Don't forget that the interview is one of perhaps three or four principal things that happen in any one hour: you still have to fit in your ad breaks, you'll be fitting in some music around the chat, there are probably other items like travel and news bulletins to consider. So, if you have a particularly busy hour, you will need to plan it carefully beforehand and create a running order of items, even if only as a rough guide. Many a radio interview has become so engrossing for the presenter that important news bulletins and ad breaks have been forgotten and not done. That would be very unprofessional.'

There then follows some repeated listening to the introduction of the next song, off-air, coupled with a serious study of the second hand on the studio wall clock.

'*Why are you listening to that part over and over?*'
'Well, I know that the intro to the next song is 15 seconds because it says so on my Selector print-out. I'm pre-fading the song and practising my next link to work out whether the bit I want to say will fit exactly into 15 seconds. In effect, I want to talk over the instrumental intro of the song. The idea is to know when the singing starts so I can shut up in time. It's also affectionately known as "jocking-the-vocal" because it's a skill traditionally attributed to disc-jockeys. Used sparingly it can bring nice effects.'

The programme has whizzed by, and it's time for the next news bulletin. But there doesn't seem to be a newsreader in sight.

'*Where is the person who's reading the news?*'
'Oh, don't worry about that. All the main news bulletins, except for the local news, are supplied to us by Network News in London. Many ILR stations take the same bulletin simultaneously. It is available on one of the faders on this mixing desk. All I do is pull open the fader at the appropriate moment, a few seconds before the top of the hour and, presto, they're there.'

After the programme, it's back to the office. Time to unwind for short while, take and make a few calls. Then start to think about tomorrow's programme. A good opportunity to take you through the mechanics of building a radio programme.

DOING THE PREPARATION

The following are general guidelines which can be applied to mainstream ILR music stations. A 'special interest' programme such as a soul or country show, which strays momentarily from the usual style of output, will rely heavily on the expert knowledge of the presenter and the music will not be predetermined by someone else.

Step 1: Study the music print-out

The programme is built around the music running order. This is the first consideration, as the music choices, more than anything else, describe the format of the station.

With radio stations becoming more format conscious, programming decisions—especially music choice—are decreasingly the responsibility of the presenter. In order for a format to be truly adhered to by all presenters, the station's output needs to be constantly monitored. So there is always a senior member of the programming team such as the programme controller or head of music listening to make sure all sounds as it should. If there were no control, a free-for-all would result, with presenters playing contrasting genres of music. Music choices that in the past at best reflected the personal preferences of the presenter, with a disregard for the listeners or format, are no longer permitted. The idea that people get jobs on the radio so that they can satisfy their own pleasures is dead and buried. You no longer choose the music you play! There will be exceptional circumstances when you will be able to liaise with the head of music to build in a music feature or make special last minute changes to accommodate the death of a famous artist, or an anniversary or in order to mention a high profile local concert. But, it is a little known fact among the general public that no radio broadcaster has played his/her own choices since the introduction in the late 1980s of computerised programme-management systems. There are several different systems in use, all with the same function, and the one you are most likely to encounter is called **Selector**.

It produces printed sheets for the presenter to work from. Each one of these represents an hour of programming. It will signpost all the important programme junctions, features and all the music you have been given to play on that day. Each song has been timed for you. All you need to know about the name of the song, the artist/s, duration, intro time and whether the song has a hard end [E] or fades [F] is done for you. Ad breaks, news and travel bulletins will also be included to guide you. It is then a case of building in your features.

Step 2: Study the permanently formatted junctions

By format junctions, we mean items that occur at the *same time* in the hour, *every* hour of the day, and in *every* programme. For instance, the news, which on some stations can appear at the top of every hour and additionally at 30 minutes past during breakfast and drivetime shows. Travel bulletins might be programmed at 20 minutes past and 20 minutes to the hour. On commercial stations, the ad breaks are also programmed at specific times, such as 10, 20, 40 and 58 minutes past the hour, religiously, every hour in the 24.

Before you can add any features, you have to calculate where those features are going to best fit in *around the format*.

Step 3: Build in the features and items of interest

You now have the outline frame-work of the programme in the music running order, formatted junctions and ad breaks. So, next you have to add some colour to your creation.

Imagine you have a colouring palette that contains an infinite variety of regular features or 'spots' to choose from. You can recognise a regular feature as it occurs at the same time every day or during the same hour in every programme. Whether it's an under-5s birthday spot, a phone-in competition, a radio dating service or guest interview slot, regular features act as further 'hooks' to interest your listeners —and keep them coming back for more! It gives you an opportunity to be creative and introduce original aspects that will attract listeners to your programme. Some features have been a roaring success and continued for years where others have fallen flat with no listener response. If this should happen, drop it quickly, without making a meal of it and think of something else. It's a good way of learning at first hand what your listeners are like.

A music feature

Items of interest in the past have included the top 10 this week five or ten years ago, a featured artist, reviews of new releases and A–Z of pop. Can you come up with something totally original?

A live guest interview

In order for this to work well as a daily feature, you will need to pre-arrange for a different guest to come in every day. This will take a great deal of organisation.

A listener participation spot (phone-in)

This type of feature always elicits a large response. Listeners really do jam the phone lines! You will need to arrange for an assistant to answer the in-coming calls or your concentration will be compromised. Listeners phoning from their cars in traffic jams, classified ads under £75, radio dating service, instant competition, stories and jokes are all ways of getting listeners to phone the programme and take part. A write-in spot works well too, but is considered rather old fashioned and slow. Listeners are less disposed to go to all the effort of sitting down to write the thing . . . put it in an envelope . . . march down to the post office . . . and queue up for a stamp.

Having said that, when someone has written you a nice complimentary letter, or asked for a birthday request, you'd do well to appreciate the effort they have gone to—please give that letter the respect it deserves and thank them on the air. Under no circumstances get on the air and respond to a complaint . . .

NB: Listener complaints are a very serious matter indeed. Never attempt to deal with a letter of complaint or angry phone-call yourself. There should always be a station procedure for this; if not dealt with correctly it can develop into a very delicate legal matter . . . accusations of slander and libel and so on. So always pass it on to the programme controller, who will seek professional advice on the station's behalf, and decide a sensible course of action. We all have the right to lodge an official complaint—without that right we wouldn't have the democratic freedom we so treasure.

Strange stories, trivia and interesting facts
Mastering the art of delivering a funny story, the results of an unusual survey or mind-boggling fact isn't easy. So many broadcasters take the easy option and will read the newspaper story or a fact from a book word-for-word. And, yes, it always *sounds* as though it's being read, with one or two stumbles thrown in for good measure. Writing that is meant to be read silently will be written in a different way to something that is going to be spoken aloud. You're better off making the piece your own. That is, re-write it, turning it into a piece that sounds like your natural flow of speech. If you find this area of broadcasting appealing, you will doubtlessly develop a liking for scanning all the newspapers, fact books and all the magazines you can lay your hands on for interesting tidbits. Remember though, it is professional courtesy to credit the author or publication when you lift news or information from another source.

You're also encouraged to use these tidbits intelligently. Taking your music selection as your framework, you should attempt to plan when exactly you are going to use them for greatest effect. For instance, you might have to play a song called 'Two Hearts'. You could spice up the show by preceding or following the song with an interesting fact about the ox or the cow having two hearts . . . (or was that four stomachs . . . ?)

A much used source of reference is the magazine *Broadcasters Q Sheet*. Containing a day by day list of historical anniversaries, famous

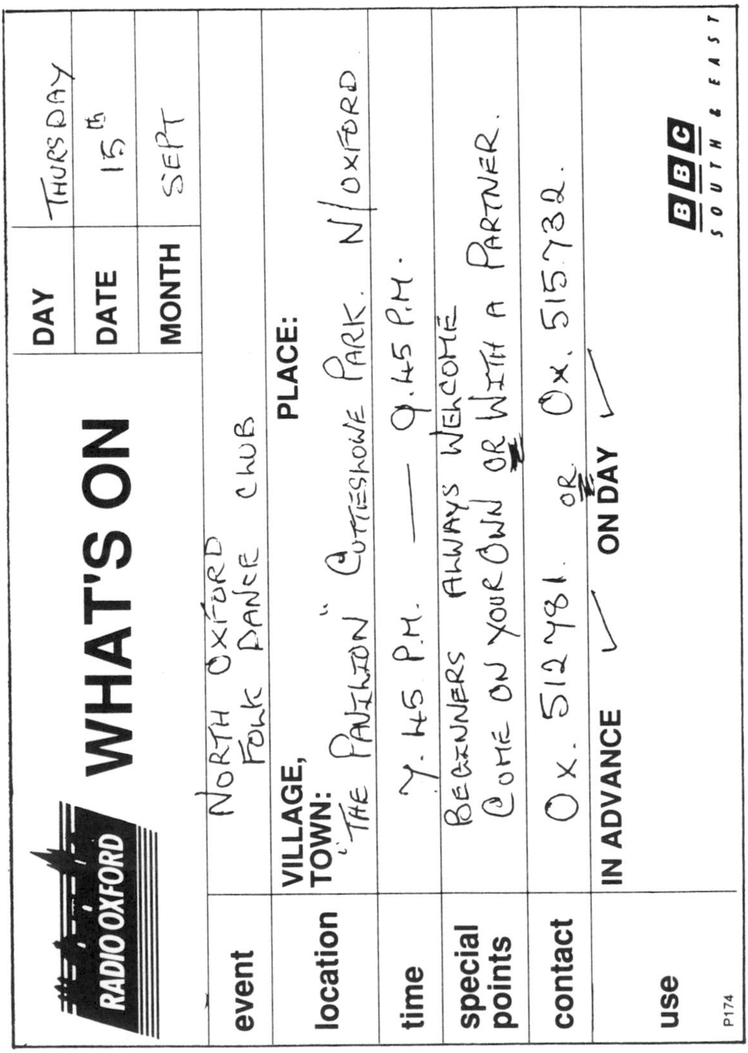

RADIO OXFORD

WHAT'S ON

DAY	THURSDAY
DATE	15th
MONTH	SEPT
event	NORTH OXFORD FOLK DANCE CLUB
location	VILLAGE, TOWN: "THE PAVILION" CUTTESLOWE PARK. PLACE: N/OXFORD
time	7.45 P.M. — 9.45 P.M.
special points	BEGINNERS ALWAYS WELCOME COME ON YOUR OWN OR WITH A PARTNER.
contact	OX. 512781. OR OX. 515732.
use	IN ADVANCE ✓ ON DAY ✓

BBC SOUTH & EAST

P174

Fig. 4. From BBC Radio Oxford's 'What's on' file.

birthdays, sunrise and tide times, interview opportunities and lots of programme prize giveaways, it's available fortnightly to broadcasters by subscription only: The Broadcasters Q Sheet, c/o Carol Dunn, The London Fox Publishing Company Ltd, 8 Wickham Avenue, Bexhill, East Sussex TN39 3EN, Tel: (01424) 732 731; Fax: (01424) 733304.

The 'what's on' diary, and local mentions

A truly local radio station, BBC or ILR, tries very hard to relate as often as possible to the area which it serves, in much the same way as a local newspaper does. Your listeners are locals, and they are attracted by the close affection the station has for the small place they know and love. Mentions of local characters they might know, shops they frequent, their schools, clubs, even mentions of small village and street names are very heart-warming. Imagine yourself as a local and listening to the person on the radio making a big deal about the lady in the corner-shop newsagent who sells you your newspapers too. You can relate: you know her too; you have to smile. Local stations feed on the local area. For instance, if you are presenting a show on a local Midlands station, it makes no sense to promote the fact that Barbra Streisand is appearing at the Wembley Arena in London. 'Who cares?' would be the response. It's a different matter if she is appearing at the Birmingham NEC. That places the event in the local area. The listener can realistically envisage arranging to go and see her.

The mention of a local event, large or small, on your programme is worth a thousand good songs. Listeners can get a thousand good songs from a national station. But, they have opted to listen to their local station for a good reason: they want to hear what's going on 'down their way'.

Every local radio station has a local events file or folder, usually called the 'what's on diary'. Left in the studio, and updated regularly by a presenter or one of the administrative staff members, it is there for presenters to use at will. You will be encouraged to dip into this file regularly. It contains short, ready-typed scripts of all sorts of local events, from car boot sales and charity discos, to local Sunday league football teams looking for new players. Most of the events and appeals are the result of the organisers themselves phoning and writing in for free exposure. Use this 'what's on' information to your advantage, it'll enrich your programme and give it a local awareness edge and convince listeners that you are interested in them and their area (see fig 4).

Step 4: Time it, time it, and time it again!

Listening to the radio, have you ever wondered why it is that songs happen to end just in time for the news jingle, followed directly by the bulletin?

From your point of view, timing is of the essence. Apart from being aware that the main news bulletin happens at the very stroke of the hour, the listener is completely oblivious of the fact that every song, every jingle, each of your spoken links has a specified duration in minutes and seconds—and every second **is** vital.

As far as the presenter is concerned, a good radio programme is not simply one that contained an entertaining interview or an exemplary selection of songs. It can also have been judged a success if, for example, all the ad breaks went out on time; if none of the songs had to be cut-off half way through to cross over to the travel news because you neglected to back-time it properly; if no ad break crashed into the news because you started it at the wrong time. An entertaining programme that was also plagued by songs crashing into ad breaks, and items not being broadcast when they should, would be a categorical screw up. Perhaps you can now also understand how a broadcaster's healthy and professional obsession with the time can lead to some characters giving out so many seemingly unnecessary time-checks; these presenters are probably constantly reminding themselves of what time it is, forgetting that it may not be all that vital to the listener. Time is everything because from now on everything is timing. The listener, however, does not need to know that you are counting the seconds.

QUICK TEST

You may be starting to realise by now that in order for items to be heard at their correct time—for example, the main news bulletin at the top of the hour—the durations of the items or songs that precede it must be carefully calculated so that they can be started with the knowledge that they will end at the right time. For instance, a song that has a duration of five minutes would not be started at 57 minutes past the hour, otherwise that song would end at two minutes into the news . . . get the idea?

Okay, suppose you were on the air. And it's twenty to ten in the morning. You have five more items to fit in this hour, the final item is the news at exactly ten o'clock. You are not allowed to drop a single item, or change the order given.

Your five items

The five items that have to be fitted in, to lead up to the main news bulletin at 10.00 are (working backwards) as follows:

5. The news at exactly 10.00.

4. The 'news-in' jingle with a duration of 15" (fifteen seconds).

3. A commercial break with a duration of 4' 30" (four minutes and thirty seconds).

2. A song with a duration of 3' 55" (three minutes and fifty five seconds).

1. A song with a duration of 5' 28" (five minutes and twenty eight seconds).

All these items have to be played-in by you, and in that strict order, leading up to the very top of the hour. You mustn't cut anything short: every song, commercial and the jingle must be played in full. In order for the last of these items, the 'news- in' jingle, to be able to fire comfortably at 09.59/45", at what time would this particular sequence have to commence? (Answer on page 147).

SUMMING UP

Actually 'driving' a radio programme can seem quite a daunting experience at first. It seems to be quite involved. Seat-of-the-pants stuff indeed! But worry not; it doesn't take long to become a master at it.

Once the basics of presenting a programme have been conquered, there will inevitably be a creative urge to invent catchy name-checks, jingles, indents and sound effects. All broadcasters go through this phase; some never grow out of it. But don't attempt to run before you can walk. Master the basics first.

A final word about having guests with you in the studio. Friends and guests are usually not allowed to sit with you. You mustn't allow your concentration to be compromised. None but the very experienced would be able to entertain a guest whilst presenting a programme, and most would not even contemplate the idea.

3
Becoming a Professional Radio Broadcaster

BROADCASTER OR DJ—KNOW THE DIFFERENCE?

The quickest way to upset or demean a professional radio broadcaster is to refer to him/her as a *disc jockey*. Part of the aim of this book is to put the profession of radio broadcasting in a good light; and to show that the broadcaster and broadcasting are not a joke.

Today's 'DJ'

In fact, today's DJ is not what s/he used to be. The term has taken on an evolution of its own. Originally, a disc jockey was somebody who, because s/he had the gift of the gab, could 'ride the discs', *ie* link the songs with a spoken message, silly joke or amusing jingle.

Case study
DJ-E-ZEE is a young club DJ. His distinctive garb gives him away. He is always to be seen wearing an obligatory baseball cap (round the wrong way, of course) and his clothes are worn deliberately four sizes too big, after an American fashion statement. His performance in the club doesn't involve chatting to the audience, cracking the odd joke or playing dedications. Rather, his particular skill is in the way that he controls the music he plays. For example, he will entertain his audience with spectacular sequences of *scratching*, that is, he physically manipulates a record on the turntable back and forth with his fingers to create a rhythm and strange effects and scratching sounds with the record deck stylus. He *mixes* records, *ie* he maintains a uniform rhythm or gradually speeds up and slows down the beat, by synchronising the rhythms of two discs and effecting an un-noticable transition from one to the other. And instead of speaking or chatting normally, will *rap*, or speak in rhyming slang, in the style of American street chat-up patter of the 1920s and 1930s, over an instrumental beat. DJ-E-ZEE is not a broadcaster!

'I aspire to being a broadcaster—not a DJ'

It's very worthwhile repeating those last words quietly to yourself until it sinks in. You are reading this book because you want to become a *broadcaster*. It's important to get this distinction clear in your mind.

There is a certain amount of confusion surrounding what it is that you're supposed to call yourself when attempting a definitive description of one 'who presents radio programmes'.

What's a 'presenter' in America?

If, after notching up some on-air experience, you feel adventurous enough to up sticks and explore a career as a radio presenter in America, make sure that your CV does not describe you as a presenter. In the USA, the term presenter is not known in radio circles and is reserved for on-screen television presenters. In America, you are a *broadcaster*. The same goes for Canada and Australia. Many Americans—but not professional broadcasters—also use the rather affectionate term of '*radio-jock*'.

More and more people in the UK who present radio programmes for a living are now calling themselves broadcasters. The most commonly used term up until now has been radio presenter.

This conveniently takes care of a multitude of sins but hasn't been a specific enough term. However, news readers and sports reporters are quite happy to describe themselves as radio journalists.

NURTURING A GOOD BROADCASTING VOICE

A clear speaking voice that can be understood by any listener is what is required.

Above all, a radio broadcaster should be fluent with the spoken word. Speech should flow naturally as it does in everyday conversation. For this reason, little attention is given to the 'mechanics' of speaking. There is no need for the future broadcaster to contemplate elocution lessons or breathing techniques. These are skills vital to an actor because acting work is more involved with 'performance' and playing characters that are removed from one's own personality. A broadcaster does not 'perform' in the same way.

Similarly, people from industries outside the arts and media, who in all probability have very dull speaking voices, may need to take lessons in technique for speaking at conferences and giving speeches, because they may not be used to speaking publicly. A broadcaster does not need to learn to 'project' his voice across a theatre or film set. Ums and ers, speaking softly and pauses might horrify a film or theatre voice coach. If a broadcaster ums and ers occasionally, it is OK because they occur in the natural speech of everyone, so long as these 'thinking pauses' are occasional and don't get in the way too much.

Other aspects of speech like inflection and stressing particular words are never used identically by everyone, and are part of your own personality. So, again, there may be only one correct way to interpret the way Hamlet speaks, which every actor has to become familiar with, but the same is not true of broadcasting. The idea is not to sound so perfectly scripted and rehearsed as to appear unnatural.

Is there such a thing as a 'male' or 'female' radio voice?

A male broadcaster should not necessarily have a rich and bassy 'voice-of-god', nor a female broadcaster sound like the sweetest, sexiest person ever born. But, if you work on the basis that the most beautiful people make it as models and film actors, shouldn't the greatest voices be the ones we hear on the radio? The opposing school of thought is that radio is supposed to act as a mirror to society, and is therefore a medium concerned with real events, rather than a fantasy world of films and fashion-imaging, and we know that not everyone in real life is blessed with a beautiful or exceptional voice. So, given that there are many men in society who have a high-pitched voice, should we not flinch at the appearance on the radio of a man with a squeaky voice?

Don't worry if you have a speech impediment

Many adults today appear to be haunted by an awful lisp, or have great difficulty pronouncing the letter 'R' to the extent that it comes out as a 'W'. It can be a weally gwating expewience for the ear.

There have been many very famous and not so famous media personalities who have sought to overcome a speech impediment, stutter or personality flaw by eventually mastering that which at first was impossible to them. This requires courage of tremendous magnitude.

Let's not kid ourselves . . . having a speech impediment means having a certain difficulty in speaking properly, or in pronouncing words the way most people ordinarily do. Interesting though the subject may be, there isn't the space here to explain the reasons why people have speech impediments. Suffice to say, there usually isn't a physical reason such as shape of mouth or length of tongue for a 'perthon having difficulty pwonounthing wordth in a shtwange way'.

You can be sure that it's all psychological and you'll overcome it once you become more confident and really start to believe in yourself.

The way you use your voice

You will really start to improve the way your speech sounds as soon as you start to listen to yourself. Listen to yourself properly, that is. You must record and listen to your programmes and be your own worst critic. Never listen to yourself straight away. Instead, leave it a couple of days, and try to listen casually as a listener—in the car or whilst doing some work at home. This way, you can listen more objectively.

Every person has a very wide vocal range. Again, confidence and state of mind can affect your voice. Have you noticed how a grown man's voice turns into a juvenile shrill when talking 'coo-chi-coo' to a baby, for instance? Or how an irritated head school-mistress's voice can boom for miles when scolding someone? We subconsciously adapt our voice to suit the occasion, mood or for maximum effect. Most men do already possess a deeper 'more manly and butch' voice than they think, but have never dared to seek it out in their vocal range. In gentle or sensitive situations, a woman will pronounce her 'Ss' in a sweeter, more delicate way than usual; it's done unconsciously and makes her appear more feminine

Is there a 'proper' way to speak?

Yes, to an extent, you could say that there is: if you can prove that there are ways in which the language should not be spoken, then there must be ways that a language should be spoken. Consider this piece of logic: a well spoken accent will be admired and looked-up to by people of all backgrounds. A rough accent or distinctly local dialect, where words are not pronounced the way our dictionaries (officially) tell us they should be, is not going to be admired by everyone.

GOING FREELANCE

Like the medieval mercenary who would be free to throw his lance for any army of his choice, being a free-lance means you have decided not to tie yourself down to one company or long-term contract. You have given yourself the freedom to make your services/talents/skills available to an infinite number of companies as and when you please, and without any contractual obligation that might otherwise prevent you from working for a number of different companies at the same time.

Generally, your services are engaged for one specific production, such as a voice-over. In the case of presentation jobs, freelance contracts are very short, usually no longer than three or six months at a time.

As a freelance you are a 'self-employed' person and you take on the added responsibilities of promoting yourself, purchasing your own equipment (*eg* professional portable tape machine and headphones in the case of a journalist), negotiating fees and processing your own billing, invoicing and tax returns.

The pros and cons of going freelance

Whilst, on the face of it, it may seem an attractive way to operate, many a freelance will speak of the reality and horrors of lack of job security, being out of work for long periods of time and waiting for payment or spending fruitless hours chasing it up.

The decision whether to go freelance isn't an easy one; the outcome either way is quite simple. If you're talented (or lucky) and find success, all well and good. If you're not, you'll suffer. Brave, or madly irresponsible, is the young man with a family to support who gambles on life as a freelance without being sure of his success.

In radio broadcasting there are many different ways to earn a living as a freelance:

- presenter
- journalist/reporter
- voice-over artist
- researcher
- electronics engineer
- computer expert
- lecturer/trainer.

Getting yourself professionally equipped

Once you have decided to become a freelance broadcaster, you will need to make a small investment and purchase some equipment of your own. Whether you are a presenter or radio journalist, having your own equipment means being professionally 'geared-up' at short notice, and not having to borrow from anyone else, or use the property of the client. A freelance photographer will have his own array of cameras, lenses and in some cases processing equipment; a freelance writer will never be without her pocket tape-recorder and home word-processor. So why should you not have your own pair of headphones, professional tape machine and editing equipment?

Headphones

Professional freelance broadcasters, including radio journalists, always have their own pair of headphones even when they have been engaged to present a programme on a long contract basis, and the station has many pairs available. Headphones that have become tatty and are shared by any number of people can be very off-putting, and probably not all that hygienic. The answer is to buy your own.

The industry favourite is the Beyer DT100. You will see these headphones in use in every radio station and production studio. The sound quality is superb, they are very comfortable, hard-wearing and very importantly, they have a 'closed' design. (Make very sure that you never acquire a pair of 'open' headphones which will feed-back on microphones, causing a nasty, piercing whistle.) The cost should not be more than £120. They are not available from high street retailers; see addresses of industry dealers in the Useful Contacts section.

Professional tape recording equipment

A professional, portable tape recording machine is an indispensable item for a freelance radio journalist and anyone interested in producing their own interview and documentary packages. That doesn't mean that a £50 personal hi fi will do the job. The fact is, any interview that you record is destined for broadcast, on-the-air. Although externally recorded pieces are eventually transferred to other tape media and made ready-for-broadcast, the original recording has to be of a sufficiently high audio quality in the first place. The original must not contain any of the nasty tape 'hiss' or other poor sound quality anomalies inherent in non-professional recording equipment—totally acceptable for domestic uses, but not suitable for broadcast purposes.

There are a number of small, lightweight, portable tape recording machines that offer the required audio recording quality and accommodate a variety of tape media. Some allow you to make high quality cassette recordings, while others will use quarter inch tape or DAT. There is also a new version of the classic Sony Walkman—the Pro-Walkman which records on perfectly acceptable quality metal cassette. If you'd like to invest wisely in your new career, and make excellent quality recordings, Sony now also market the new portable Walkman DAT (around £400), and the excellent MZ-R2 Sony MiniDisc Walkman (around £450).

The most popular broadcast quality tape machines used by radio journalists are models manufactured by the companies Marantz, Uher and Tascam. Prices between £400 and £1200 new.

Tape editing equipment

You may already have some experience of editing tape in your own home studio. But if you need to hire a studio to produce your own feature or put together a montage of interviews, you are best advised to have your own tape editing materials.

First, get yourself a large and robust pouch or pencil case, then fill it with the following:

- **An editing or splicing block.** This is a heavy, solid metal block measuring approx 20cm x 5cm. It has specially cut grooves to edit (join) two pieces of tape together, plus razor blade grooves for different angle edit cuts.

- **Splicing tape.** Similar to Sellotape or insulation tape, splicing tape is white sticky tape on a tiny roll. It's used to make the physical tape edit. Specially designed for easy removal if an edit isn't quite right.

- **Editing blades.** Believe it or not, there is never an editing blade to be found in the studio when you need one. The one you eventually do find is either rusted, blunt or full of Chinagraph lead. The type used is similar to an old fashioned razor blade but specially designed for the purpose of cutting audio tape. Do yourself a big favour and purchase a box (around £6 for a box of 100).

- **Chinagraph pencils.** You may already have come across this type of pencil as it's also used to write on chinaware and glass. Its thick, soft lead will be either yellow or white, and is very suitable for marking tape for edit cuts (around £6 for a box of 12).

The equipment described above will not be available in high street shops. Contact the following radio industry suppliers for a catalogue (for addresses see the Useful Contacts section):

Canford Audio, tel: (0191) 415 0205 also produce a 'starter editing kit', comprising a selection of the aforementioned (around £17).

Studiospares, tel: (0171) 482 1692.

Promoting yourself as a freelance

As a freelance, you are a self-employed person in every sense. In essence, you are your own company. It means that as well as being approached by others and having offers of work made to you, you also have to take it upon yourself to make yourself known to radio stations and production companies in the hope that they may have work for you. In fact many companies do not often need to advertise their vacancies, because they will already keep a file containing the availability, CVs and demo tapes of the freelances who have contacted them.

In the salesman's vernacular it is known as the 'cold-call'. You make approaches to companies, for the first time (ie cold), either by telephone or in writing, with the idea that if they don't have a vacancy at the present you will be leaving with them information about yourself, a well-made demo tape and CV, so that when they do have to engage the services of a freelance, they can quickly and easily assess your suitability.

Never forget that you are in constant competition with a number of other freelances who are equally as talented and able as you are—and just as eager to work. The first impression you make with any company must therefore be good, if not exemplary. Otherwise the details that they 'promise to keep on file' will not be.

Getting a professional letterhead

You're calling yourself a professional broadcaster, but are you making this blatantly obvious every time you write to a company? Virtually every company has a specially designed logo which appears on their letterheads, compliment slips and so on. And although you don't have to go as far as having a specially designed logo, you do need to make a slick and professional impression. You are your own company, remember?

All freelances who care about being taken for a serious professional have a personalised letterhead. It is simply having your name, address and telephone number printed in a stylish manner across the top of your letter or typing paper. Consider the kind of impression that a non-professional approach will make. For instance, a letter typed on a blank sheet of paper, with your address typed on the top right and the company's on the left. Or, even a letter that has been hand-written on a blue, lined Basildon Bond writing pad. 'This is not from a professional', will be the immediate reaction.

You can have your letterheads printed inexpensively at an instant print shop like Kall Kwik or Prontaprint. There will be many lettering styles to choose from. Alternatively, you may have your own desk top publishing system, in which case you can create your own. You will be giving your written applications and correspondence a polished, professional and business-like appearance that will command respect.

Producing your demo tapes
This is such an important topic that an entire chapter has been devoted to it—chapter 5 'Getting Your Demo Tape and CV Right'.

Opportunities for the voice-over artist: radio and TV
A voice'over is the spoken dialogue which you might hear on a commercial, nature documentary or training film. The voice-over artist is never seen, only heard. None but the very best voices are used. The men and women who are gifted with exceptional voices are very highly sought after. They can demand very high fees: an hour's script-reading can pay as much as £500, even in the case of a short radio commercial when the voice-over lasts only 20 or 30 seconds. The most successful voice-over artists are people like the actor Andrew Sachs ('Manuel' in TV's *Fawlty Towers*), who is well known for voicing nature documentaries, and his son, the broadcaster John Sachs (TV and radio commercials), the actor Martin Jarvis, Ian McShane (TV's *Lovejoy*), the actress Joanna Lumley, Capital FM presenter Chris Tarrant, and so on. Whilst the most lucrative voice-over work is taken by the big name actors and well-known TV personalities, there is still an enormous market for the rest of us.

Many a broadcaster who has found success in voice-overs has decided to retire from presenting altogether to concentrate on working only as a voice-over artist, voicing radio and TV ads, promotional videos and documentaries.

It is one of the ways you could be giving your regular earnings a good boost. Remember to request a copy of every voice-over you're asked to do: the better ones can contribute to future voice-over demo tapes.

The audiotext information and entertainment industry

Audiotext is the technical name for premium rate telephone messages/ programmes. Members of the general public who need flight departure information, the latest FT index update, sports results or a tarot card reading will phone a special number for which they are charged around 50p a minute.

This medium is still striving to achieve the good reputation it deserves after suffering the indignity of a number of disreputable companies promoting less than tasteful pornographic entertainment on their lines. Nevertheless, the audiotext industry exists and will continue to do so for the foreseeable future, providing voice work for thousands.

The following audiotext associations will put you in touch with the service providers (the companies who make the programmes) who may be in need of voice-over artists:

Association of Telephone Information and Entertainment Providers (ATIEP), c/o Elaine Garrod, 3rd Floor, Russell Square House, 10-12 Russell Square, London WC1B 5LF. Tel: (0171) 637 1696; Fax: (0171) 637 1697.

The Independent Committee For The Supervision Of Standards Of Telephone Information Services (ICSTIS), c/o Arabella Martin, 3rd Floor, Kingsbourne House, 229-231 High Holborn, London WC1V 7DA. Tel: (0171) 430 2228; Fax: (0171) 831 4474.

Joining broadcasting associations and clubs

Whilst many radio professionals never bother to join a broadcasting society, association or union, assuming it to be a waste of time, many others have managed to make new friends and useful contacts outside of their usual circle of friends and close community of work colleagues.

Unlike unions, whose function is to defend the rights of employees and campaign for fair pay and conditions and so on, professional 'clubs' are formed with the purpose of bringing together like-minded people to further knowledge and understanding of the craft, to foster new talent and offer the benefits of their combined wisdom and experience to those who need it.

It can be quite lonely working as a freelance. Making friends, exchanging ideas, forming close associations with people who have similar aspirations can only help you in the long run. It would be well worth your while if you would enjoy attending social evenings, seminars and talks on radio.

At a time of great change and expansion, it would be of particular benefit to you to keep in close contact with radio station associations such as the Community Radio Association, and Association of Independent Radio Companies (see chapter 10, Seizing the new opportunities).

Broadcasting associations

Community Radio Association: (Head office) 15 Paternoster Row, Sheffield S1 2BX. Tel: (0114) 2795 219; Fax: (0114) 2798 976.

(London office) Vauxhall Centre, Belmore Street, London SW8 2JY. Tel: (0171) 738 8788; Fax: (0171) 720 7518.

The Radio Academy, PO Box 4SZ, London W1A 4SZ. Tel: (0171) 323 3837.

USING A STAGE NAME

It hasn't been proved that one person's chances of success are better than another's because of their name. It isn't even correct to assume that people with very contemporary English, Irish, Scottish or Welsh names do better in Britain than those with a foreign name: Paul Gambaccini, Steve Lamacq, Mark Tonderai, Mary Costello, Sujata Barot, Petroc Trelawny and Mariella Frostrup are just some examples of successful broadcasters who have a foreign name.

Do I need to change my name?

It's a question that will cross your mind, particularly at the outset of your career. The answer is no. But you are free to do so if you don't like your present one. Putting family pride and your roots aside, you could ask yourself the following:

Has my name always attracted ridicule?
Don't let your name handicap you. You really don't have to remain saddled for the rest of your life with a comical surname like 'Wigglesbottom', for example.

Is my name difficult to pronounce?
You may be endowed with a name from eastern Europe, which may have an interesting derivation but contains combinations of letters that most other people don't know how to pronounce, like 'Krzyzscz'. Or, an equally exotic Asian name like 'Amwrallindusticanavr', which would also present most people with problems. It's time to be brutally honest with yourself. If you have the slightest doubts about your name, have no qualms—change it.

Researching the most popular radio names in use

Your name, for example, might be Joanna Stevens . . . there may already be three other Joanna Stevens working in British radio, so you might want to change yours to avoid confusion. You can conduct your own survey of the names of all British radio broadcasting personnel including presenters and journalists. It is a good idea to check that your name, even if you're happy with it, isn't already very common. There are currently 23 Clarkes, 31 Davies, 45 Smiths and 66 Joneses presenting on British radio. It may in fact be advantageous to have a very popular or common name—it is yet to be proved either way. The choice is entirely yours; follow your heart.

The *Blue Book of British Broadcasting* (£38–£40, or ask your library to get it for you) is the source for this information; published yearly by Tellex Monitors Ltd, Communications House, 210 Old Street, London EC1V 9UN. Tel: (0171) 490 1447; Fax: (0171) 490 8595.

Changing your name by deed poll

There is no law preventing you from calling yourself anything you want, and working and earning money under that name—other than for a wilfully criminal act like fraud or impersonation, of course. You are quite free to exercise your imagination and invent a stunning new name like Scott Davenport, Ashley Conrad or Lindsey Brahms.

Many self-employed people including freelance broadcasters don't feel the need to officially register their assumed or 'stage name'. Strictly speaking, you don't need to. Changing your name by deed poll may have its advantages, though, if for any reason your claimed identity is brought into question. And opening back accounts, getting credit/store cards, buying property, registering votes and so on may be made easier.

A deed poll is simply '. . . a formal deed which is dated'. There is no mystery or complicated legalities concerned with changing your name by deed poll. This is how you go about it:

Step 1 Go to a solicitor (it doesn't have to be any specific type of lawyer). S/he will conduct the entire process from initial enquiry to completion.

Step 2. You will then be asked to sign a sworn declaration. There is a small 'swearing fee' to pay—under £10.

Step 3. You wait only a couple of weeks, after which you are notified that the registration process is complete. And you have a new name.

Your name for bank accounts

One of the reasons why registering your name by deed poll is a good idea is that providing banks with adequate proof of identity can be difficult. If you do decide to work under a stage name or pseudonym, make sure of opening at least one bank account in this professional name. Unless you have issued special instructions for payment, you will receive payment in the form of cheques payable to the name you work under (imagine the tedium of having to do this every single time, '. . . actually, that's my stage name, not my real name, could the cheque be made out to . . .'). You will not be able to pay it into any bank account other than one which is operating in the same name.

GETTING AN AGENT

The primary function of an agent is to find you work in return for a percentage of the fee s/he has managed to secure for you. This is usually 10%, although this does vary according to the agent, the type of work in question and length of contracts and so on.

How an agent can be useful

You may be a creative talent or skilled journalist and good at what you specialise in, but it doesn't necessarily follow that you would be good at selling yourself. An agent can describe you to others in glowing terms, probably more effectively than you could. Also, an agent, if s/he is good, will already have placed other talented people with radio stations and organisations and will have made those all-important contacts with the decision makers. Because an agent is constantly representing people and in daily communication with 'the field of work', s/he will be very well-informed as to what work is available (they are also the first to hear about other individuals who may be unhappy and want to move on, or one whom a station wants to replace—situations which create new vacancies).

If you're fortunate enough to get an agent who truly cares, s/he will be able to give you advice on the ways in which you can improve yourself. Nobody is perfect, so listen very carefully when it's experience talking to you. An agent can also negotiate the best terms and contracts and do all the haggling over fees and salaries: in effect doing your dirty work for you! Many professionals who battle it out on the job market without any professional guidance, especially those new to the business, are so delighted just to be offered a job that they often agree to any fee that is mentioned—unknowingly falling victim to a skilled negotiator of fees who has just saved the company some money, and earned himself a few brownie points for getting you a little cheaper. The only time you will ever see the words 'business' and 'honesty' sharing the same sentence is this one.

Finding the right sort of agent

This is crucial. If you need an agent who is used to nurturing new talent like yourself, then it's very simple—find an agent who's used to handling new talent like yourself! Steer clear of those agents who will take on just about any type of entertainer: the 'all-round' agents who handle dancers as well as singers, variety and circus acts, ventriloquists, and extras who appear in *The Bill*—as well as radio presenters. Unless you can be convinced that the agency does have someone who specialises in your field, you will be wasting your time with this type of 'general entertainment' agent. You need to focus specifically on the area of radio in which you want an agent to find you work. Then seek out those agents who specialise in that area. There are agents who only have a client-base of serious high-brow presenters who specialise in politics, or only female voice-over artists, or specialise in very young 'Pop DJs'.

Keeping your agent up to date

When you have been fortunate enough to find an agent willing to take you on, treasure that relationship. Telephone every couple of weeks and keep them up to date with your movements. Having an agent doesn't prevent you from making your own efforts to find work, but tell your agent the moment you do. You may also be liable to pay the agent a percentage of fees even if s/he wasn't in any way involved in the negotiations.

Try to furnish your agent with as much information about yourself as possible. Keep the agent fully supplied with ample copies of your demo tape/s, CV, publicity sheet, newspaper clippings/magazine write-ups, radio and TV interviews, photographs and so on. These are the very tools which the agent will skilfully use to 'sell' you; without any of this, the task is made all the more difficult.

The following agent and artiste yearly directories have acquired bible status in the industry. Consulting these in your search for the right sort of agent is a must:

The White Book (published in the spring): Birdhurst Ltd, PO Box 55, Staines, Middlesex TW18 4UG, England. Tel: (01784) 464441; Fax: (01784) 464655.
Show Call: The Stage Newspaper Ltd, Stage House, 47 Bermondsey Street, London SE1 3XT, Tel: (0171) 403 1818; Fax: (0171) 403 1418.
Spotlight on Presenters (contact: Jan Younger): *The Spotlight*, 7 Leicester Place, London WC2H 7BP. Tel: (0171) 437 7631; Fax: (0171) 437 5881.
The Presenter's Contact File (contact: Colin Cobb): Presenter Promotions, 123 Corporation Road, Gillingham, Kent ME7 1RG. Tel and fax: (01634) 851077.

COMING TO RADIO FROM A RELATED FIELD

Many people from related fields have succeeded in bringing their interesting talents, useful knowledge and experience to radio. So, if

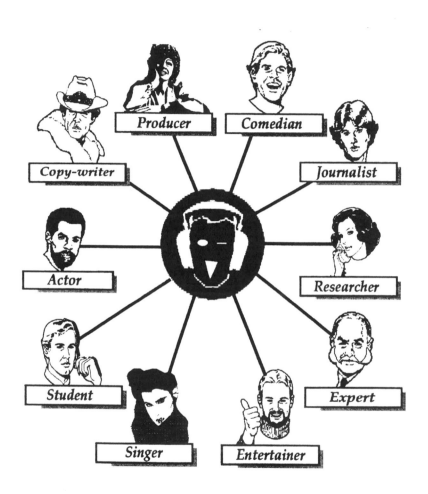

Fig. 5. Coming to radio from a related field.

you're a newspaper reporter, actor, singer, press officer, commercial copywriter, comedian, club DJ, after-dinner speaker, PR consultant, drama student, compere, TV producer, researcher, stadium announcer or audiotext (telephone programmes) voice-over artist—and have a good measure of common sense and a genuine desire to communicate through the magical medium of radio, then a career as a broadcaster is well within your grasp (see fig 5).

SUMMING UP

In this chapter, you have learned:

- To appreciate the difference between a broadcaster and a DJ.
- How to become a professional freelance broadcaster, and market yourself as one.
- How to go about getting the right type of agent, and how to change your name legally if you wish to do so.
- How welcome you are, if you're coming to radio from a related field.

CHECKLIST

1. If you're considering applying for a radio job in America, don't forget to make sure that your CV does not say you are a 'presenter'. They don't use this word in American radio, and might confuse you for a TV presenter. Remember to include the word 'broadcaster' in your CV.

2. You can cast aside any worries about having to take elocution lessons to work in radio. There's no acting in the radio presenting biz—just be yourself; we love you just the way you are.

3. So you love the idea of becoming a freelance. Have you started thinking about getting properly geared up with your own headphones, recording and editing equipment?—you could get an offer of work out of the blue!

4. Remember, to be regarded seriously as a 'professional' you must remember to write to companies on personalised letterheads.

5. Would you like to have an agent find work for you? Then you must get hold of the 'agent directories' listed on page 47.

4
Getting Started

FINDING A STARTING POINT

'How do I get a job on the radio, then?'

Now, there's a familiar question! If high ranking agents, radio stations and established broadcasters had a penny for every time a would-be broadcaster phoned up out of sheer desperation to ask this direct question . . . In fact, alarm has been raised in the radio industry at the number of people who express a keen interest in working on the radio without having made any effort at all to realise their ambition. These enquirers form the largest core of people who want to make a career in radio and they're actually serious about it.

They could be bringing their interesting talents to an industry that is increasingly on the look-out for new blood, if only they knew where to get started. But in the main they haven't got any relevant qualifications or training, nor can they claim to have even a limited amount of DJ-ing experience, much less display a vocational passion for radio. It's as though people have come to the conclusion that there might be some mystery to it, and to get that illustrious job on the radio you have to be extremely lucky, or happen to be in the right place at the right time, or know the right people who will get you in.

Becoming a radio broadcaster isn't the result of a rare fluke, but is well within everybody's grasp and you can make it happen for yourself. The important thing to understand is that you have to get started somewhere. Nobody starts their career presenting a top-flight national breakfast show.

Sooner or later the day will come when you will have to take the plunge somewhere and slip on a pair of headphones, get behind a microphone and start to practise your craft. The dilemma that faces employers and prospective candidates alike is how to pit having qualifications but no real hands-on experience against having a limited amount of experience with no training to demonstrate an interest in progressing onto the next level. Each individual approach will be unique: get some formal training first and delay slipping on a pair of headphones and getting on with it. Or forego any formal training and get stuck-in straight away. There is little doubt, though, that when an employer is faced with having to decide between hiring someone who only has a little experience, and a qualified person who has never actually 'done it' before, the choice will be academically in favour of the candidate who has already started to earn a living talking into microphones.

It has to be said though, that the BBC have always had a slight bias towards a high standard of education over talent or artistic bent, in both TV and radio. This is why from time to time we see or hear someone on the BBC who knows their subject inside out but who definitely doesn't have a 'radio voice' or, in the case of TV, doesn't have any 'presence'. For the sake of the craft, this would seem to be the wrong ethos. To answer the questions already forming in your mind: the radio is first and foremost an entertainer, after that it is all the other things like educator and informer. It would be easier to listen to a beautiful voice talking nonsense than an adult male, however expert in his field, whose child-like squeal grated on the ear. Both are irritating in their own sweet way.

Where do I start, then?

If you've never even spoken into a professional microphone before, you will need to get your career started somewhere. There are many levels where you can enter radio—you can either start working as a disc jockey and blossom gradually into a professional broadcaster. Or if you're already a club DJ or are coming in from a related field and have some relevant experience, you can start your broadcasting career on another level of radio—a parody of the real thing but where the techniques, approach and dedication to the craft are the same. Like hospital radio or in-store radio.

Your age, family circumstances and current job, career or whether you are in the middle of a degree course will have a bearing on which route you take. You may not want to throw away everything you've worked for in the present job (if it's completely different) and take a blind chance on radio only to discover that it's not for you. You may want to work in professional radio only on a part-time basis—such as at weekends, while continuing to pursue your career. This is fine: a full-time commitment is not mandatory. But remember that what you put in will equal what you get out of it. So your advancement may take longer. You may already have made a start and want to discover other rungs on the radio broadcaster's ladder: areas in which to add to your experience.

Case study—Mike Rophone, 26

'I began disc-jockeying as a "bedroom mixer", making up compilation mix tapes for friends. From this, I was asked to entertain people at birthday parties and private functions. I soon discovered that I had more than an aptitude for conducting audience-participation games and keeping people happy by playing the music they wanted to hear.

'A friend who was a resident DJ at a local fun-pub introduced me to a DJ booking agent, well-known in the area for providing DJs in a whole circuit of pubs and clubs. I expressed an interest in gaining some work experience in the types of venues where there was an opportunity to communicate with the audience rather than those places where people just want to dance. After a few trials I was given regular nights at local fun pubs and clubs where I learned a lot about microphone technique and different styles of music.

'I spent a year as a pub DJ, always knowing that I would be moving on and getting closer to achieving my dream of working in radio.

'The next step was hospital radio. So, I booked myself into a professional production studio and set about making a demo tape. I had a good idea of what to put on it, and the guys in the studio were experienced broadcasters themselves, and they gave me a few tips.'

The traditional way into radio

There is a traditional, well-trodden path into radio which many of today's professional broadcasters have taken. You don't have to follow this route strictly, because, as you will see, you can start 'DJ-ing' or enter radio at various different levels. You might use the following as a guide:

- Step 1. DJ-ing at a pub, club or with a roadshow

- Step 2. Becoming a hospital radio volunteer

- Step 3. DJ-ing on in-store radio

- Step 4. Working on a 'pirate radio station' (this activity is illegal and you are strongly advised to avoid any participation with the pirates—see below)

- Step 5. Becoming a local BBC or ILR broadcaster

- Step 6. You get head-hunted by Radio 1 or Capital Radio . . . followed by overnight fame, fortune, TV and having babies named after you.

This is by no means the only route in and you can enter radio at various levels. But showing you this classic route is a perfect way of demonstrating that there is a variety of ways of serving that vital 'radio apprenticeship' . . . of sorts.

NOTCHING UP SOME VALUABLE EXPERIENCE

Those of us who're so keen to make it into radio, start DJ-ing or break into radio at another lower level, and progress from there—we can work our way up. Whether you are an absolute beginner or have already made a start and are edging yourself ever closer to getting that on-air job you've always hoped for, there follows an introduction to all the places you could be notching up some valuable experience.

DJ-ING IN DISCOTHEQUES, PUBS AND CLUBS

Of all the places where you can start notching up some DJ-ing experience, pubs and clubs are the most popular. You can find work even if you have little or no experience at all. Sheer enthusiasm may get you a break here.

Getting the right sort of DJ work

Remember to keep your goal in focus. You are working towards becoming a broadcaster; one who actually communicates coherently in modern everyday conversational English through a microphone for everybody to understand. So, the sort of DJ work you should be looking for is that which will give you the opportunity to learn how to use a microphone to chat and converse and play a variety of music. Learning how to mix to the beat and rapping in a badly imitated American accent will be of no use to you whatsoever as a broadcaster —the only exception to this rule being that you might be interested in specialising later on in dance and club culture.

Making your debut

One way to make your debut is by joining a mobile discotheque or roadshow as an assistant. There'll be a lot of heavy equipment to lug around and little or no wages, but you could be given the opportunity to 'have a go for the first time'. Being able to say you've worked on a mobile disco will ring familiar bells to a club owner and will show that you have some relevant experience. Another way is to make friends with a club DJ and persuade him/her to let you try your hand at it; perhaps before the club opens or when it's not too busy. You may well get the opportunity to fill-in while the DJ takes a break for half an hour. This could lead to getting your own regular 'nights', 'sessions' or 'residencies'.

Finding disco work through agents and agencies

Perhaps the best way to secure work in clubs is through an agent or agency who will be contracted suppliers of 'jocks' for a 'circuit' of clubs of varying sizes and audiences. You would be working to an itinerary organised up to a month ahead with bookings in a variety of establishments.

For addresses of DJ agencies, see the Useful Contacts section.

Making sure DJ-ing is definitely for you

If you're motivated by pop music and take your energy and inspiration from following the record charts and are generally oriented towards the youth culture of pop concerts, fashions and pop videos, the perfect arena in which to 'open that mic fader' for the first time is in a club or pub.

Learning the basics

It's a good place to take your first and inevitable stumbles (you won't even need a drink for this). You'll learn how to use a microphone:

- Not speaking directly into it has no effect at all
- Shouting into it will result in a distorted sound
- Speaking too closely to it makes a muffled sound.

You'll hear how your voice sounds:

It can be an amusing experience the very first time. How many people swear blind that, '. . . it cannot be me . . .' if shown a video of themselves, for instance. You'll make improvements to the way you speak. You'll learn:

- How to project your voice
- How to change the inflection of your voice
- How a smile can be heard in a voice
- How to grab people's attention
- How to sound authoritative

You will learn by instant reaction how playing 'Don't cry for me Argentina' will not be very well received by the mother whose young son died in the Falklands war, and she was having a good time up until the point you decided to play it without exercising sensitivity.

You'll learn to appreciate the versatility of a mixing desk and how to control the sound levels.

You'll be introduced to record turntables, and you will learn how to cue records. CD machines and tape recorders may also be in use in some clubs.

You'll widen your appreciation of different music styles.

Doing the right thing

- Don't drink and make a fool of yourself
- Project the image of the club in a good light
- Always be on time
- Be polite
- Dress smartly
- Pay your income tax and national insurance contributions if you are self-employed. There are a number of accountants who specialise in dealing with the tax affairs of disc jockeys and entertainers. They offer excellent advice, and may even be able to save you a substantial amount of money. They advertise every week in: *DJ Magazine, The Stage & Television Today* and *Broadcast Magazine*.

The Inland Revenue will catch up with you many years later if you avoid paying tax. Even if you work under a stage name the companies you work for eventually have to pass onto the authorities the names and details of all the people they have employed—that's how they catch up with you.

Discover whether you are an entertainer

People go to pubs and clubs to relax and unwind from the pressures of work and to forget their complicated lives for a while. They momentarily 'stop the world and get off'—and they expect to be entertained by you. Whether you make them laugh, are a smooth-talkin' soul sister or whether you are a talented purveyor of musical trivia—working in pubs or clubs will teach you a little bit about how to entertain people.

The word 'entertainer' frightens a lot of people. Don't worry if you're not a natural comedian or showman: keeping people 'entertained' in the purest sense means keeping their minds 'diverted' or having them pay attention to something for a while. You may discover that you are a natural entertainer. What you learn here will remain with you and will come in useful later on. If the sort of broadcasting you eventually intend to pursue is going to be of a more serious, analytical nature, like journalism or 'talk radio', you will not necessarily need this grounding in entertaining. What you will get out of it is a good basic introduction to microphone technique and a useful introduction to audio equipment.

Choosing where to work carefully

Most pubs and clubs attract a decent, well-mannered clientele who will enjoy listening to you, forgive your beginner's errors and even offer you kind and gracious encouragement. But it would be prudent to be selective when it comes to deciding where to work. As soon as you are offered the work, a good move would be to visit the place for a drink beforehand as 'mystery customer': a good way of assuring yourself that you would feel comfortable working there.

For a list of magazines which give a good coverage of the DJs, clubs and discos spectrum see the Useful Contacts section.

DJ-ING OVERSEAS IN 5-STAR HOTELS

Could you wear a tuxedo and bow-tie?

The plush and sophisticated environment of a Hilton or Inter-Continental hotel discotheque lends itself to having a well-spoken, educated DJ/host who would feel at home in a glitzy tuxedo jacket and equally spectacular bow tie.

Exciting contracts in Europe and the Middle East

You are contracted to work as the resident hotel club DJ. Contracts can vary but they are usually either three, four or six months at a time (renewable if they are happy with you) depending on the contractor. As well as developing as a DJ, you'll be widening your horizons. Your posting could be to Germany, Sweden, the USA or even somewhere exotic like Bahrain.

In most cases you are offered the option of taking a room in the hotel which you are not charged for. Your meals in the hotel are free, either new records are sent out to you once a month in places where up-to-date music might be difficult to get hold of, or an allowance is provided for you to buy records locally and add to the club's collection if the location is a modern international city. And all travel expenses are met by the contractor too. Because practically all your living expenses are found and you don't need to spend any money on records, the remuneration won't amount to much more than extra 'pocket-money', ample to enjoy yourself in your free time.

Getting in some radio practice

Usually, the music from the club will also be piped through to all the hotel's rooms and elevators in the evening and be available to the guests as one of the music channels, giving you the opportunity of presenting a low-key radio show of sorts during the early quiet hours, inviting guests to '. . . join us later this evening at Hamiltons, our roof-top night-club on the seventh floor here at the Inter-Continental because we're having a party and we'll be rocking 'till three am!'

A cocktail bar atmosphere

The typical up-market hotel club discotheque will have a cocktail bar atmosphere about it. The clientele will be made up mostly of travelling business men and women socialising and entertaining guests on generous expense accounts. The local well-to-do and even the occasional Arab princess with her entourage of 30 personal maids! These are people who expect the best possible service and can afford to pay for it. All clients are waiter served. When a guest buys you a drink, it will most likely be a glass of champagne, and a record request scribbled on the foreign currency equivalent of a £20 note would not be unusual.

Perfect for the glamorous female DJ

This sort of club requires a DJ who can be something of a charming, attractive host. It is going to be far easier for a female DJ to meet this criterion of glamorous appeal, and so girls are usually the preferred choice. But this should not deter any cultured, stunning-looking guys from approaching the DJ agencies specialising in this kind of work.

The 'international hotel discotheque contractors' (DJ agencies) to contact:

London Town Discotheques Sound & Lighting Ltd (contact Joanna & Peter Van Pragh), 80 Wandsworth Common, North side, London SW18 2QH. Tel: (0171) 385 5521.

Juliana's, Suite 2A, Long Island House, 1/4 Warple Way, London W3 0RQ. Tel: (0181) 749 4939.

Expo Entertainments, 22 Cols de Sables, St Brelade, Jersey, Channel Islands JE3 8GJ. Tel: Jersey (01534) 41649; Fax: Jersey (01534) 41649.

Gary Brown Associates, (Hilton International Entertainments), 27 Downs Side, Cheam, Surrey SM2 7EII. Tel: (0181) 643 3991; Fax: (0181) 770 7241.

ENTERTAINING ON CRUISE LINERS AND FERRIES

Are you the all-singing-and-dancing type of DJ?

This is the perfect stepping-stone to radio for people who come from a related field in the entertainment business such as dancers, singers and entertainers.

Being a versatile entertainer

DJs working on board cruise liners will also be expected to join in with the other entertainment activities like putting on shows and cabaret. If you can sing, dance and are a general all-round entertainer who is willing to get involved with every aspect of on-board entertainment, this is for you.

On-board radio stations and discotheques

If you are an all-round entertainer/DJ with ambitions in broadcasting, working on a cruise liner will also offer you the opportunity to operate the on-board radio station. Just as in hotels, it is piped into the cabins, restaurants, shops and recreational quarters.

A typical day might see you presenting a radio programme in the morning, joining in with a matinee performance in the afternoon, and DJ-ing in the discotheque that same evening. Although your radio work will be largely un-supervised, you will get an excellent opportunity to make something of a start on your broadcasting career!

DJ-ing on European ferry lines

On the shorter ferry sailings—around the British Isles, Ireland, northern France, Holland and Scandinavia—there is no call for having an on-board radio station. But many shipping lines do have a discotheque on their ferries, making for further openings for DJs.

Getting DJ work on ships through specialist agents

It is best to approach any of the following DJ agents rather than shipping lines direct:

Britannia Entertainments & Promotions, Victoria House, Paxton Street, Hanley, Stoke-on-Trent ST1 3SD. Tel: (01782) 219595; Fax: (01782) 202133.

Ian Clark Entertainments, 20 Blackwall Road, Ashford, Kent TN24 0NU. Tel: (01233) 635422; Fax: (01233) 612958.

Brian Layne Management (contact: Angie, Kim or Steve), 43 Tamworth Road, Copnor, Portsmouth, Hampshire. Tel: (01705) 754543.

Mr Gray's Entertainments, (Cruising & International), 188/192 Station Road, Westcliff on Sea, Essex SS0 7SB. Tel: (01702) 345000; Fax: (01702) 347217.

Scott Paul Young Entertainments Ltd, Northern Lights House, 110 Blandford Road North, Langley, Near Windsor, Berkshire SL3 7TA. Tel: (01753) 693250; Fax: (01753) 810961.

BECOMING A HOSPITAL RADIO VOLUNTEER

'Is it *real* radio?'

With the exception of 'Radio Phoenix (Neath Hospital Broadcasting)', which in 1988 was granted permission by the Radio Authority to start broadcasting a low-powered FM signal that locally can be picked up on 95.7 MHz FM, this type of radio isn't real radio per se.

Who listens to hospital radio?

Hospital radio exists for the benefit of patients who are either awaiting or are recovering from an operation or other treatment. This type of radio is a cable-delivered service, piped in a closed-circuit fashion to the wards and staff restaurants. The patients are able to listen in using headphones which hang on every headboard, beside a socket and volume switch (see fig. 6).

Today's top professionals started on hospital radio

The vast majority of broadcasters have begun their radio careers on hospital radio. Many who began here have continued their involvement in hospital radio, often 'scouting' for new talent within this medium. Sir Jimmy Saville OBE and Noel (Crinkly Bottom) Edmonds are two good examples.

Entering hospital radio from a clubs background

If you want to get into hospital broadcasting from a clubs background, you will do well to think very carefully about the difference between a hospital radio audience and a club. Your talents for being able to create a 'party atmosphere' in a club, for instance, will be about as useful as a chocolate teapot on hospital radio.

Hospital radio is the place that you can learn to develop from DJ to broadcaster. Whereas in clubs, volume of music, mixing to the beat, projecting your voice—to shouting point (and even telling dirty jokes!) were important considerations, you will realise that in radio these things don't apply. Other things become important, like:

PROGRAMME GUIDE

Riverside Radio aims to provide a wide range of programmes 7 days a week for listeners exclusively in Charing Cross Hospital. Our programme schedule changes four times a year on the first Monday in September, December, March and June. There are also special programmes for Christmas and New Year.

The programme Guide on the following pages gives a general guide to what's on. Our aim is to provide all the programmes at the times stated but, inevitably, we will not be able to all the time due to volunteers being unavailable. When we are not 'on air' BBC Radio 2 provides a sustaining service, ensuring 24 hours a day, 7 days a week, of the very best in entertainment. So stay tuned to Channel 2 whatever the time of day.

MONDAY

2.00 pm	**Two in the Afternoon**
5.00 pm	**Early Show with Alan Kenny**
	Music, your requests and dedications, plus news of the day
7.00 pm	**Music Feature**
7.30 pm	**Bingo Show**
	Tommy and the team bring you our weekly prize game which you can play from the comfort of your bed!
9.00 pm	**Late Show with Tim Davies**
	Late night music and requests on the ligher side to wind down the evening
10.55 pm	**Thought for the Day**
11.00 pm	**As Radio Two**

TUESDAY

2.00 pm	**Two in the Afternoon**
5.00 pm	**Early Show with Sarah Greenwood/Claudia Bryan**
7.00 pm	**Golden Decades with Dave Phillips**
	The music of the 1940s and 1950s
8.00 pm	**Two's Company**
	Our weekly magazine programme with Shakeel Ansari and the team
9.00 pm	**Late Show with Sean Quinn**
10.55 pm	**Thought for the Day**
11.00 pm	**As Radio 2**

WEDNESDAY

2.00 pm	**Two in the Afternoon**
5.00 pm	**Early Show with Shakeel Ansari**
7.00 pm	**50 Plus with Clive Rosolin**
7.30 pm	**Russel Annear**
	With your requests and dedications
9.00 pm	**Late Show with Roy James**
10.55 pm	**Thought for the Day**
11.00 pm	**As Radio 2**

THURSDAY

2.00 pm	**Two in the Afternoon**
5.00 pm	**Early Show**
7.00 pm	**As Radio 2**
	(Note: Thursday evenings are usually used for radio training of our members, but from time to time additional programmes will run through up to 11.00 pm)

FRIDAY

2.00 pm	**Two in the Afternoon**
	Katrina Lindsay and Melissa Buckley bring you an afternoon of news, special guests, your requests and of course some great music!
5.00 pm	**Early Show with Mike Scott**
7.00 pm	**Nice 'N Easy with John Henty and Friends**
	Chat, interviews and features programme produced in association with British Telecom
7.30 pm	**Jeremy Honer**
	With your requests and dedications
9.00 pm	**Late Show with Frank Tobin**
10.55 pm	**Thought for the Day**
11.00 pm	**As Radio 2**

NEWS—regular updates throughout each day on the hour

Fig. 6. Extract from a hospital radio programme guide.

- being able to communicate well
- presentation slickness
- working and talking to strict timings
- widening your knowledge of music until it covers *all* types and styles, including classical, jazz, country, pop and rock.

No songs about death please!

Your listeners are sick patients. Some of them are suffering great pain. Some are near death, and very sad. Each station will have their own music policy. But it would be the sensible future broadcaster who exercises a degree of caution over music choice. Clearly, songs that in any way are about 'death', like the Rock 'n' Roll classic—'That'll be the day that I die' by Buddy Holly, or Queen's 'Bohemian Rhapsody' which contains the lyric '. . . mama, (I) just killed a man' are totally unacceptable. Even the *Mail On Sunday* thought it newsworthy enough to report in July 1994 that Dudley District Hospital Radio in the West Midlands censored Frank Sinatra's 'My Way' because of the line in the song '. . . And now the end is near, and so I face the final curtain . . .'

A good introduction to news and journalism

As well as presenting a variety of music programmes you might develop an interest in journalism. The opportunities will be there to learn how to:

- prepare and present local news magazine programmes
- conduct interviews
- package features
- how to splice and edit recorded speech.

Your first introduction to radio studio equipment

There is an array of audio machinery and equipment which you may not yet have come across working in clubs.

- Mixing desks that are rather more complex than those used in clubs
- Broadcast microphones
- Broadcast headphones
- CD cart machines
- Broadcast turntables
- Jingle cart machines
- Open-reel tape recorders

- Professional portable cassette and tape recorders (used to record interviews on location).

Note: Hospital radio stations are voluntary organisations and rely to a large extent on the generosity of record shops and record companies for an up-to-date supply of music. BBC and commercial stations updating various equipment with new models regularly donate second hand studio equipment. It may be comforting to know that the equipment you'll work on has already been used by professional broadcasters to broadcast 'real' radio programmes.

Always remember you are a volunteer
Any work you do at a hospital radio station will be unpaid (you may discover that some stations can pay your travelling expenses, but it would be the exception rather than the rule). The idea that hospital radio stations can carry advertisements has in recent years added an exciting twist. Certainly, there already exists a hospital TV network (Medic Media in association with Thorn EMI and the NHS have developed a nationwide TV network which carries adverts for medicines and treatments, and is available in hospital waiting areas).

Further news and general information are available if you reach out to the (nice) people at the country's main governing body in hospital broadcasting: NAHBO (National Association of Hospital Broadcasting Organisations), Milne House, 1 Norfolk Square, London W2 1RU. Contact: Aileen Faulkner on (0171) 402 8815 or : Colin Powell on (01324) 613 744.

Ask the person at NAHBO to help you find those hospitals nearest to you which have a radio service, as you're very interested in sending a demo tape.

NAHBO also publishes a regular house magazine called *On Air*.

BROADCASTING ON CAMPUS RADIO

Campus radio, college radio or university radio provides the student with a perfect stepping stone to professional broadcasting. A sizeable number of universities and colleges around Britain operate this type of low-key radio. Broadcasting from within the grounds, it is run by students—for students. Many uni-radio stations are being granted experimental RSL licences (see 'Getting a break on restricted service radio', in this chapter). If you are a student planning to go to university anyway, and have your ambitions partly set on broadcasting, it might bias your choice of college knowing that it might also have a radio station where you can get involved in your free time. Network Chart host Neil [Dr] Fox began his broadcasting career on University Radio Bath. For more information on Campus Radio, contact: The Student Radio Association, (Andy Tennant: chairperson). Tel: (01602) 513617; Fax: (01602) 790017.

BECOMING AN IN-STORE RADIO DJ

Another excellent place to improve your presentation skills and prepare yourself for professional broadcasting is in-store radio. These work on the same technical principle as hospital radio. In- store radio is another parody of the real thing: operating in a closed-circuit fashion for the benefit of customers as they shop in the store. The presenter sits in a fully equipped studio booth inside the store and in full view of the shoppers. As with hospital radio, the style of presentation, approach and quality of programming make in-store radio a dead-ringer for the real thing in many instances.

You're entertaining young shoppers
We're talking youth-market retail here, aren't we? So, shoppers to these types of stores will in the main be young, teenage and very fashion-conscious. As the in-store radio DJ you will be providing background music and chat, voicing live commercials advertising the store's products, so you also become the focus and part of the attraction. In assessing your own suitability for this type of working environment you'll have to decide whether you would enjoy, or indeed are properly cut out for, working to a storeful of young ladies like the enormously trendy Top Shop stores around Britain. You'll also discover in-store radio stations operating in the more fashionable of the record stores, like HMV in Oxford Street, London. You might be called on to interview a top name band live in the store and get involved in other such record company promotional activities, so you need to be 'chart aware' and be prepared to play almost any type of music.

Some celebrities who started on in-store radio
A good number of today's top radio professionals worked on in-store radio before moving on to bigger things. To name a few: Children's BBC TV presenter Andy Peters and Steve Collins of Capital FM & Jazz FM fame both worked at Radio Top Shop. And Virgin 1215 presenter Nick Abbott started his broadcasting career on Virgin Megastore radio, in Oxford Street, London.

The companies to contact:

(For Top Shop London, Liverpool and Manchester) Fashion FM Ltd (contact: Peter Knott), Air Play Music, 214 Oxford Street, London W1N 9DF. Tel: (0171) 636 7700.

Radio HMV, HMV Records, 150 Oxford Street, London W1N 0DJ. Tel: (0171) 631 3423.

Virgin Megastore Radio (VMR) (contact: Clinton Bell), The Virgin Megastore, Oxford Street, London W1. Tel: (0171) 631 1234.

ASDA FM (National In-Store radio) (contact: Jerry Rowlands), The Studio, Spring Bank, Astley, Manchester M29 7BR. Tel: (01942) 896111; Fax: (01942) 884397.

Grand Central Network (Commercial cable radio for the retail trade in Newcastle and Sheffield) (managing director: Wayne Chadwick), PO Box 516, Sheffield S3 7FB. Tel: (0114) 2725273.

GETTING A BREAK ON 'RESTRICTED SERVICE' RADIO

Restricted services, also referred to as 'special events radio' and 'festival radio' are legal stations, fully licensed by the Radio Authority and PRS (the Performing Rights Society) to broadcast for up to 28 days at a time.

Well over 200 restricted services a year are given permission to set up as a radio station that meets the professional requirements, and broadcast to a locality covering not more than a radius of 25 miles. In order to maximise publicity, stations such as these might typically choose to broadcast for the duration of a local 'festival month', provide coverage of Hampton Court Flower Show, for example, or in the run-up to Christmas, thereby making the most of lots of interview and outside broadcasting opportunities.

Helping a new station gain a full licence

These stations are permitted to broadcast in an experimental way under the watchful eye of the radio governing bodies. The aim is to make a good impression on the likes of the Radio Authority so as to make a good case for retaining a permanent licence to broadcast as a community station.

This is where you come in. By getting involved with programmes and helping with outside broadcasts, you not only get some useful broadcasting experience under your belt, but you could also be helping the station gain a permanent licence when at some point in the future the Radio Authority announces that the area should have a local station—perhaps securing yourself a regular programme slot at the same time. Please note that because these services hope to capture the true 'flavour' of a given locale, preference will be given to interested parties who live in and are familiar with that area.

The official bodies responsible for issuing broadcast licences will tell you which restricted services are setting up, where and when:

The Radio Authority (contact: David Vick, head of development), Holbrook House, 14 Great Queen Street, London WC2B 5DG. Tel: (0171) 430 2724; Fax: (0171) 405 7062.

The Performing Rights Society Ltd (contact: Norman Dodd, deputy manager), Broadcasting Liaison Dept, 29-33 Berners Street, London W1P 4AA. Tel: (0171) 580 5544; Fax: (0171) 631 4138.

BROADCASTING ON COMMUNITY RADIO

Community means more local than 'local'

Community radio is the nearest thing to local radio, except that this type of station serves a significantly smaller audience—perhaps 450,000 people. A community radio station is a permanent on-going commercial concern, broadcasting a general mix of music programmes and local news coverage regulated by the Radio Authority. In the main it is controlled by the community it serves, with all the profits it makes from advertising being used to develop its programmes.

Community radio works closely with social action groups and local charitable causes. Some stations are commercial and therefore able to employ full-time staff; others are run by volunteers—you can regard this type of radio as one which offers you a golden opportunity to notch up some on-air experience. If you decide to join a voluntary community radio station your involvement would be similar to that on hospital radio, but with a 'real' radio audience—and ten times as large, as that.

Some good examples of community radio:

1. RTM Radio (Radio Thamesmead)

This station serves the south east London community. Broadcasting from studios within a housing tower block in Thamesmead Town—a 1960s new town, rather like Milton Keynes. Talking of which . . .

2. CRMK (Community Radio Milton Keynes)

As with RTM Radio, this station first went on-the-air in 1990. As well as broadcasting on an FM frequency, its programmes are available to people living and working in Milton Keynes via cable TV audio channels. As one of the few exceptions to the rule, CRMK is staffed entirely by volunteers. Its audience numbers some 200,000 people. It is the longest serving community station in Britain, beginning its transmissions as a cable-delivered service in 1979.

3. North East Community Radio
This is a cable-delivered community service serving the Aberdeen area of Scotland. It broadcasts a non-commercial 24-hour service which is run by volunteers.

In some cases community means 'ethnic' community, catering for a local Asian or Afro-Caribbean society. Here are some examples:

1. Radio Harmony (Coventry)
2. Spectrum International Radio (Greater London)
3. Sunrise Radio (Bradford, Leicester and Southall)
4. Supa AM (Birmingham)
5. Turkish Radio UK (London)
6. LGR (London Greek Radio)
7. Radio Orient (London cable community radio)

It could be your first 'big break'
Anybody who has some experience either as a DJ or preferably hospital radio or in-store radio could well be making their radio broadcasting debut on community radio. As with special events radio, a good proportion of its programming will be slanted in favour of reflecting the people and lives of the community it serves—a familiarity with (or great knowledge of or enthusiasm for) the locale is always appreciated.
The official body concerned with the development of community radio to contact for further information: The Community Radio Association, The Media Centre, 15 Paternoster Row, Sheffield S1 2BX. Tel & fax: (0114) 279 5219.
Community Radio Association (London development unit), Lambeth College, Belmore Street, London SW8 2JY. Tel: (0171) 738 8788; Fax: (0171) 720 7518.

PIRATE RADIO BROADCASTING

Q. Should I join a pirate radio station?

A. It cannot be stressed enough that you must never contemplate becoming a radio pirate. It is highly illegal, and any participation whatsoever, be it running the station, presenting programmes or selling air-time, carries very stiff penalties including imprisonment. You may even find yourself 'blacklisted' by the Radio Authority, making it virtually impossible for you to approach any legally operating stations for work in the future.

Q. Weren't most of today's big names pirates once?

A. Of course, it is a well-known fact that many famous voices, from Tony Blackburn and Kenny Everett to Pete Murray and Dave Cash, all began as DJs on the pirate ships such as Radio Caroline and 'Big Radio London'. However, you have to remember that it was the 1960s and there was a distinct lack of radio openings for the new-styled pop radio broadcaster. In fact there were none. No pop stations at all. British pop fans and the new providers of this new genre had to wait until 1967 to get its first pop music station—Radio 1.

So, the radio pirates appeared, deciding they would just do it anyway, whatever the government thought. The idea initially was to embarrass the government of the day into realising that they could not prevent people for ever from broadcasting this brand of popular commercial radio in Britain, at a time when there were already hundreds of pop radio stations in America, for example. Most pirate stations had made formal approaches for a licence, to no avail. There is then a sense of 'justification' for the actions of the early pirates.

But there's no excuse for someone having to resort to joining a pirate radio station any more. It has clearly been proven that today's pirate radio organisers are frequently linked with other criminal activities as well. Imagine being caught and named as an accomplice in other crimes; your career would be over before it even had a chance to get started! We have nigh on 200 radio stations in Britain now. We will see at least a further hundred new stations start broadcasting before the millennium. Opportunities for new radio broadcasting talent abound. Forget all about pirate radio!

Note: The term 'pirate radio' is generally taken to refer to illegal broadcasting. This term, however, in no way acts as a description for, nor should it be confused with, the ILR station called 'PIRATE FM 102.2', which is a fully authorised and licensed commercial radio station serving the Cornwall, Devon and Isles of Scilly areas.

CHECKLIST

1. Remember to target your demo tape (see chapter 5 'Getting your demo tape and CV right').

2. Assess your suitability carefully.

3. Before you approach an agent familiarise yourself with the piece on agents in chapter 3 on 'becoming a professional'.

4. You should not concern yourself with buying your own equipment or records—look for work where these are provided. Being a DJ will only be a passing phase, jobs that will act as stepping stones to the 'real thing'.

5. If you are offered an overseas job, make sure to ask the company for rules and regulations on visas, work permits and inoculations (in the case of tropical countries). And is your passport up to date?

6. In the case of club work, try to obtain a written agreement (on starting, don't rock the boat beforehand; ask the employer for a letter—say it's for your accountant's records) which describes without question or doubt the terms, hours of work, fees and so on. Verbal offers of work can easily be broken (or be misunderstood).

7. Honour your contracts and agreements.

8. Don't forget to **have fun**!

5
Getting Your Demo Tape and CV Right

MAKING SURE THEY LISTEN TO YOUR DEMO

It doesn't matter how good you are. Not even how good you think you are or your friends passionately insist that you are. If your demo tape and CV package has the slightest hint of a shoddy unprofessional manner about it, it probably won't even get looked at; they will use your cassette to record an album for the car, and not even read the CV . . . heart-breaking so let's get it right!

Being aware of the competition

Think back to what you are aspiring to be—a broadcaster. A professional broadcaster, at that. Your demo and CV package is going to be competing with those from other broadcasters . . . who already know the rules of the game. So if you're going to stand any chance of getting an airing, you're going to have to try as hard as them—if not harder.

It isn't just novices wanting to break into radio, looking for a programme controller to give them that merciful 'first big break', who send in demo packages to radio stations. There is a constant stream of pitching from established pros who may simply want to relocate, or from those who have been working in radio for a few years and are looking for a better time-slot after serving a few years on the dreaded overnight 'graveyard shift'. Your first chance at 'real' radio could well mean working an anti-social shift. It's very exciting, and you welcome the break with open arms, but as anyone who has done it will confirm, the novelty of staying awake to present through the night soon wears off. Don't be put off but official scientific study reveals that you are at your 'lowest ebb' at 04.00 (regardless of how much sleep you get during the day) and going against the biorhythms for prolonged periods can do serious damage to the nerve endings. Agree to do it for a year at most, or until your finger pads start to develop a strange fizzing, tingling sensation!

PUTTING YOUR ABILITIES ON SHOW

Your hopes and dreams, your very chances of breaking into radio, are going to rest above all on your demonstration tape. It's the broadcaster's version of the actor's 'show-reel' or 'audition tape', the means by which you are going to put yourself, and your abilities on display:

- quality of voice
- personality
- intelligence
- reading abilities
- maturity
- attitude towards others and life in general
- expertise or interest in a particular subject

And faults?

No. Never give the impression that you're capable of making a mistake.

Your demo tape must show you at your best

You're not happy with mistakes so why sell yourself on the premise that you are. Many novices assume they will be ingratiating themselves if they ascribe to showing their 'human side' and include or let a few 'mis-takes' or stumbles go while reading. You're going to be hired on the basis that you can do the job well—not vice versa. The purpose of the demo is to show you at your best.

What about political views and sensitive subjects?

There are many views as to how neutral the media's stance should be, and actually is, with regard to politics. All newspapers and news programmes are to one degree or another politically biased. If you decide to include an interview with a Conservative politician only, the less open minded listener might get the wrong impression about your feelings, no matter how you deal with the feature. The way around it is to include a balance of views. The reality is that you cannot appear totally neutral without giving all views a fair hearing. Remember that the demo is not a critical soap box. Speaker's Corner in Hyde Park, London is the place for that. You are trying to get a job. You may take your chances with a politically slanted joke but you could be running the risk of slandering someone without realising it. Err on the side of caution.

Play it safe

When considering what you are and are not allowed to talk about on the radio, it would be wise to swot up on what the Radio Authority has to say about comments on politics, slander and subjects of a sensitive nature. Knowledge of this area of media law is an entire study area all its own, and very deep. Not only useful to radio journalists but all broadcasters. The Radio Authority publishes very clear and easy to understand guidelines for you to keep and refer to later on.

Phone them and ask for the following booklets:

1. *Radio Authority Programme Code 1*—News programmes and coverage of matters of political or industrial controversy or relating to current public policy.

2. *Radio Authority Programme Code 2*—Violence, sex, taste and decency, children and young people, appeals for donations, religion and other matters.

The Radio Authority, Holbrook House, 14 Great Queen Street, Holborn, London WC2B 5DG. Tel: (0171) 430 2724; Fax: (0171) 405 7062.

CHOOSING THE RIGHT TAPE FORMAT

The first sensible thing to do is to visualise the intended listener to your demo tape. S/he will invariably be a very busy person with very little time to spend listening to tapes.

What equipment will they use to listen to my tape?

This is an important consideration when choosing a tape format for the demo. In a radio station full of state-of-the-art broadcast and production studios, it might surprise you to learn that the typical programme controller has in his/her office nothing more complicated than a very small and simple stack hi-fi, and very often only a portable radio cassette player. This is sufficient in order to be able to monitor the output and listen to tapes.

Which *tape* format should I use to record my demo onto?

The following tape formats are acceptable:

● Cassette

1. Offence to Good Taste and Decency and the Portrayal of Violence

1.1 Language

The gratuitous use of language likely to offend must be avoided. Bad language and blasphemy must not be used in programmes specially designed for children or broadcast in circumstances such that children might be expected to be listening (see paragraph 1.4).

There is no absolute ban on the use of bad language but its use must be defensible in terms of context and authenticity. It is one thing, for example, when such language occurs in a documentary programme, and quite another when introduced for its own sake in, for example, a music based, entertainment programme. Many people who would not be unduly shocked by swearing are offended when it is used to excess and without justification.

1.2 Sex

The portrayal of, or allusion to, sexual behaviour must be defensible in context and presented with tact and discretion. Smut, titillation, crudity and sexual stereotyping must be avoided.

Overt sexual conduct between humans and animals and between adults and children must be transmitted and can be referred to in programmes only after consultation at senior radio station management level.

The same considerations apply here as to bad language. Popular entertainment and comedy have often relied to some extent on sexual innuendo: but this does not justify smut, titillation, mere crudity, the portrayal of perversion, sexism, or the degradation of either sex. Much of the world's great drama, music and fiction has been concerned with love and passion, and it would be wrong (if not impossible) to require writers or lyricists to renounce all intention to shock or disturb: but the aim should be to move, not offend.

1.3 Bad Taste in Humour

(a) JOKES ABOUT PHYSICAL DISABILITY

Such jokes need to be considered with great care on every occasion.

The roots of laughter are often found in deviations from the normal and familiar. But there is a danger of offence in the use of humour based on physical disability. Even where no malice is present, such jokes can all too easily, and plausibly, exploit or humiliate for the purpose of entertainment. This not only hurts those most directly concerned but can repel many listeners.

(b) RACIAL JOKES

Jokes based on different racial characteristics may offend. Licence Holders must be sensitive to public attitudes to what is and is not acceptable.

Although it may be unlikely a joke would constitute an offence under the provisions of section 6 ('Incitement to racial hatred') of the Race Relations Act 1976, it may nonetheless offend against good taste or decency or be offensive to public feeling.

(c) RECORDED ITEMS

Items not used immediately must be checked before transmission to ensure that jokes or scenarios are not rendered tasteless by intervening events, such as death, injury or other misfortune.

1.4 Children and Young Persons

The Radio Authority believes that adult radio listeners have the right to enjoy material which would not be thought suitable for children. However, Licence Holders must be aware of circumstances such that large numbers of children and young persons might be expected to be listening. These circumstances prevail at the times when a Licence Holder regularly directs his programmes at children and young persons by the inclusion of music, stories or speech items acknowledged to be specifically attractive to [them].

Fig. 7. An extract from the Radio Authority broadcasting guidelines.

- DAT (digital audio tape)
- Open reel quarter-inch

Why recording on cassette is best

You are best advised to present your demo on a cassette, especially as you are going to make it as easy as possible for the programme controller to listen to it. The cassette format is very versatile. Some controllers with busy schedules even listen to tapes in their car. There is nothing stopping you sending in a quarter-inch tape reel, but think about the controller who most likely doesn't have a reel-to-reel machine in his/her office, will probably have to book a production studio or interrupt somebody who is already booked in. S/he then has to re-configure the mixing desk settings and inputs which might have been altered for a previous production. S/he has to lace-up the tape. And finally s/he gets to hear you. It may literally be many days before your tape is listened to.

The same goes for DAT—a much lauded tape format, not least for its CD quality reproduction, but again the hunt would be on for a machine to use. It makes far more sense all round if s/he is able to pop a cassette in. Don't be too concerned about the cassette offering inferior audio quality compared to the other formats. It's a good opportunity for the controller to hear what you would sound like on a small radio which is what most listeners use anyway. If you can impress them on a small unit, you're obviously going to sound superb on a sophisticated hi-fi—a good test to pass. Also, if the station happens to be a Gold format, it would be broadcasting on AM anyway and 99% of listeners would be listening on a small portable.

The radio journalist demo tape

Only deviate from the above if you are sending a demo tape to a different department. You may want to apply for work as a reporter, in which case your demo is going to be aimed at the head of news and features or current affairs. The general news department scene is one of an open plan area strewn with open reel tape machines, with headphone-wearing reporters and journalists poring over a news item or feature, quickly editing and splicing their copy in time for the next bulletin. So, given this working environment, radio journalists are better off presenting their demo on an open reel.

The voice-over artist demo tape

If it's voice-over work you are pitching for, your tape is going to be offered to a different department head—Commercial production in this case. This department produces, writes and records commercials.

Because of the importance of commercials and large sums of money involved, quality control is at a premium. The medium here is CD (for sound effects and short instrumental music beds) and DAT. Commercials that are produced 'out-of-house' and supplied by advertising agencies mostly come in on DAT format. So, if you plan to step into the lucrative world of voice-overs, put it on DAT.

How a CD could be very useful

Recording your demo onto a CD would be original and certainly impressive, but expensive. It's not at all impossible to arrange with a growing number of independent recording studios offering this service. A one-off CD can be recorded for about £60–80. Many radio pros use a compact disc to keep a personal collection of features, live links and interviews. Most of us eventually end up with important material that we want to keep to use for future demos, but it is often strewn about the house, on different tape formats and on videos and so on. Where the CD comes into its own is that you can store up to an hour of recordings on one disc—making storage and locating pieces to transfer to cassette swifter than ever.

GETTING THE RIGHT CASSETTE MATERIALS

Having decided on the correct tape medium to record the demo onto, you must make sure that the blank tape is of a professional standard. Not just in sound quality but also in presentation.

Many newcomers to radio can be forgiven for not knowing that it is possible to achieve a more professional presentation than simply recording the demo onto a TDK, Memorex, Sony, Maxell or other high street retailer manufactured C-60 or C-90 cassette.

What should the duration of the demo be?

Generally speaking, the duration of a demo tape should not exceed ten minutes. Shorter if possible! If your demo is going to be of a short duration, it follows that using a blank tape with a duration of half an hour or even 45 minutes makes little sense and gives the impression that you might be an uninformed and inexperienced 'outsider'.

Short duration tapes are available from several professional radio industry suppliers. Although they don't advertise they are always pleased to help members of the general public and newcomers to radio.

Cassette durations

Blank cassettes are available to people wanting to effect a professional presentation in all durations—from C-5s (five minutes) up to C-120s, graduating in intervals of five minutes. But, think very carefully before you order. If your demo is going to run a duration of ten minutes, a C-10 is not going to do the job. Remember that a C-10 cassette will mean five minutes each side! You must therefore decide on a C-20 or C-30 to play it safe.

Customising your own cassette labels

To complete your professional visual presentation, you will need a supply of unmarked labels. Industry-supplied audio cassettes are available in all the colours of the rainbow; the most common are black and are not labelled or marked. The labels are white. It's a perfect opportunity to smarten up your presentation by typing or laser printing your details onto the labels. They come in A4 size sheets of ten labels or on a roll for you to peel and stick on. If you have the opportunity you can slip the sheets into your typewriter or computer printer.

Resist the temptation of making your labels look like a magazine holiday advert, however artistic or talented a desk top publishing expert you are. Having said that, we are after all, working in the entertainment business, so if you can achieve a professional business-like impression and at the same time manage a hint of expression and colour, that's fine.

What information needs to appear on the label?

You must include the following:

1. Your name (stage name or performer name if different from your name at birth)

2. Your home address and phone number

3. The duration . . . for example six minutes and 37 seconds. In broadcasting, duration times are written in shorthand: a single (') apostrophe denotes the number of minutes, and a double (") apostrophe indicates the number of seconds. So *six minutes and 37 seconds* becomes 6' 37"

4. The date. What is important is that the date which appears on the cassette is the same as on the covering letter. The idea is to avoid giving the impression that your tape is an old production. You

may have conceived the idea for the production one or two years earlier, and its contents are still just as valid, but nobody needs to know that or be put off by this fact. Instead, always give it a fresh, up-to-date, 'just recorded especially for you' feel. (Fig 8 shows examples of the wrong and right way of presenting your demo.)

Mass-producing your demo is not a good idea

You should avoid taking the lazy route and prepare ten or twenty generic tapes to send out 'mail-shot' fashion. Of course, you only need 'one lucky bite' to succeed, so why not take your chances? But is this really the way of the pro? Are you showing that you've conducted a little bit of research, surveyed the market, and actually found out something about the station you are applying to? No. And it will show.

Note: There are two main distributors of professional audio equipment and supplies in Britain. They also deal with hundreds of overseas enquiries every week because they are world renowned in the industry. Call, write or fax them both for a catalogue:

Canford Audio, UK sales, Crowther Road, Washington, Tyne & Wear NE38 0BW. Tel: (0191) 415 0205; Fax: (0191) 416 0392.
Studiospares Ltd, 61/63 Rochester Place, Camden Town, London NW1 NJU. Tel: (0171) 482 1692; Fax: (0171) 485 4168.

WHERE TO RECORD YOUR DEMO TAPE

If you're not sure where to go to record the demo, it's a good idea to study (very carefully) the pages of these trade and entertainment magazines where independent production studios regularly advertise:

● *Broadcast* (out Friday)
● *The Stage & Television Today* (out Thursday)

Also highly recommended:

● *The White Book* (published yearly in the spring) Birdhurst Ltd, PO Box 55, Staines, Middlesex TW18 4UG. Tel: (01784) 464441; Fax: (01784) 464655. (It is the industry 'bible' and is not available in shops. Price: around £43.)

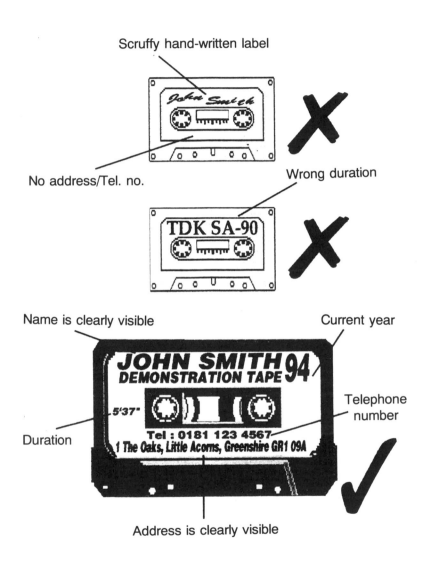

Fig. 8. The right way to a professional looking demo tape.

If you are unemployed or a student, ask your local library to get these publications for you.

PUTTING TOGETHER YOUR FIRST DEMO

Preparing a script and a running order

In the early stages you should aim to display a 'general' awareness of radio. Even though you may be completely inexperienced, you can at least show you are a radio listener and have a grasp of what is required. You're not expected to sound professional if you've never done it before, so don't worry if you don't turn out sounding as polished as you know you can eventually. We all have to start somewhere. What would please them at this stage is to hear a good attempt.

You are going to construct your own running order of about ten items. Each person has their own way of expressing themselves and uses different words, so you don't necessarily have to follow the example word for word—do 'busk' around the script given, in your own way. For the sake of this demonstration, we shall assume that the station is of a general entertainment format with a good mix of speech and music content.

Step 1 (I introduce myself)
'Hullo, Middlesex Hospital Broadcasting welcomes you to another evening of programmes. This friendly voice belongs to (. . .) and I very much hope that over the next three hours we have something for *you* . . .'

Step 2 (I play a song)

Step 3 (I read a weather forecast)
Note: because of local variations in weather forecasts it would be more sensible if you transcribed a forecast from your nearest station and used that. On no account tape any station's jingles (from the radio) to use on your demo. It could turn into a very complicated area involving copyright and even impersonation.

Step 4 (I play a song)

Step 5 (I read a short news bulletin)
Note: do as you did for step 3.

Step 6 (I play a song)

Step 7 (I give a run-down of programmes)
'Well, as I mentioned earlier, I'm here until nine tonight . . . then after the news it's an hour of jazz with (. . .), followed at ten tonight by . . .'

Step 8 (I play a song)

Step 9 (I read a request)
Make up a 'congratulatory' dedication to someone, eg someone who's just passed their exams or driving test.

Step 10 (I say my goodbyes)
'Thankyou for being there. I look forward to your company next time around . . .'

Editing your recording to the correct length

Take control over the production of the demo
Once you have recorded the links complete with songs, you have to 'top-and-tail' the songs. This you must do as a professional courtesy. It means you are going to ask for the main chunks of the songs to be taken out. There are two good reasons for doing this. At this stage the demo is far too long. Secondly, there is no point in the programme controller having to hear the songs in their entirety when listening to your tape—s/he already knows what they sound like, and s/he wants to hear *you*.

Case study—Ray

Ray Dioman, 24, didn't bother to target his tape . . .
Ray is a relative newcomer to radio. He has been a volunteer on his local hospital radio station and has learned a lot about presentation techniques, and he is looking forward to experiencing the full excitement of broadcasting on a 'real' station. In the two years that he's been helping out at the hospital radio station, Ray has had the chance to present a variety of programmes, and has developed a liking for rock music. He eventually gets the urge, feeling he's ready for a whirl at presenting for the national rock station Virgin 1215. Ray decides to record his demo tape at the hospital radio station, and luckily he has kept recordings of the different programmes he has presented in his time there: country, jazz and rock shows, request shows, community news magazine supplements and so on.
He finally records his demo. When he sends it off, it contains ten

different snippets from previous programmes. Of the ten, there is only one link that features Ray commenting on a classic rock album before he is heard playing a track from it. The rest of the demo has Ray making mention of a local girl guides jumble sale, setting the scene for a George Hamilton IV country music hit, and reading a long-winded local news story—none of which would be of any interest whatsoever to the typical Virgin 1215 listener, and which would never form any part of their programming.

Assessment
Ray made the grave mistake of not even listening to Virgin 1215 to see what kind of music they play and what topics might be of interest to the listeners. Ray learned the hard way that he was wasting his time and effort in sending 'any old demo'. In the case of a station like Virgin 1215, a station with a very definite programming remit targeted at an age group of people with specific musical tastes, interests and lifestyles, you have to study them as much as you can so that you can tailor your demo tape to suit. In essence, Ray's demo tape should have been made to prove to the programme controller that Ray was right for Virgin 1215. Therefore, Ray should have already 'visualised' himself as a Virgin 1215 voice and produced something that would bear a very close resemblance to what is already heard on that station. There's no point in showing that you're proficient in something that's not needed. Nor is there any call for trying to change the world by daring to be different . . . just yet.

PREPARING YOUR CV

There really is no hard and fast rule as to the way a CV should be presented. The information you include is the most important. The amount of information that your CV contains and what form it's going to take will depend on how experienced you are.

Be creative and design your own—this way you will be expressing your personality at first contact with a prospective employer. Never hand-write it, however nice your writing is. Always type it or have it laser printed. And it should not be longer than one sheet of A4 size paper, using both sides if necessary. Try to include the following information:

Personal details
Your name, address, telephone number, nationality, date of birth, place of birth, and marital status.

Education and qualifications
List all your exams and grades, and dates you took them, and name all the schools and colleges. Be sure to mention any radio training or media qualifications.

Employment details
If any, try to stress any work you have done that might be relevant to radio. Otherwise keep work details very short, as it will be of very little interest if you have been a tree surgeon or driving instructor for the last three years.

Interests and hobbies
Generally, candidates don't make the best of a good opportunity to show what kind of a person they are. Your hopes, passions, temperament, ambitions and life driving-force are truly revealed in your sparetime interests. Nobody would waste their spare time on activities they didn't enjoy. So your sparetime activities reveal what you're really about.

Clearly, a programme controller would want to see in you a passion for media related topics and activities. Such as stating, '. . . I am very media-aware. I read various newspapers, listen to a variety of radio formats, and enjoy watching news and current affairs discussion on TV'. Sounds good, doesn't it? But, you had better be telling the truth: you may well be asked to describe what you read and listen to, at interviews.

Getting the image right
All too often, CVs are received from broadcasters that give completely the wrong impression. Many CVs give the impression that they might in truth be sent by a chartered accountant because the CV simply doesn't scream BROADCASTER, or at the very least, someone who belongs in the arts and entertainment business. To a lesser or greater degree, there is in all of us, in this business, an artistic flair and temperament. (For reasons that nobody can fathom, photography seems to be very popular among broadcasting people.)

Express yourself!
People who perhaps don't work in the entertainment and media business give general 'expert' advice on how to present your CV— advice that warns against preparing a CV that looks too 'flashy' or 'you should avoid colourful packaging'. Good packaging shows professionalism.

Newspapers, magazines, brochures and company documents these days all contain more colour and text effects. Colours are a fact in nature and all around us. We now have the technology to create some stunning documents, so what is the problem? Let your CV be your calling card. If you are a flamboyant person, then express it in your CV! By all means, have it designed on a computer DTP system using all manner of colours and text effects. There isn't a hard and fast rule that dictates what your CV should look like. If your personality reflects a quieter, more reserved, intellectual nature, let your CV contain only two colours . . . or just black on white without any text effects. If you are able to, include a photograph . . . who was it that said, 'a picture is worth a thousand words'?

Make the best of the new technology
Various computer software packages now exist that allow for a 'picture still' to be taken from a video cassette. Conceivably, your CV could have superimposed on it a colour picture of you in the studio in action.

Letters and letterheads
Unless you are a calligraphy specialist or a professor of graphology, type your letter. (See page 41.)

WRITING A WINNING LETTER

Always find out the name of the person you're writing to; 'Dear programme controller' or 'to whom this may concern' only shows that you're not all that bothered if it reaches the right person. If you are applying to stations for the first time you should keep your letter short and to the point. (See the example on page 84.)

THE DEMO DOS AND DONTS

Do
Record your demo at a proper recording studio.

Don't
If you're a club DJ, record it on your disco unit, or send in a recorded example of an evening at the club. The functions of the club DJ are very different to that of a broadcaster.

Don't
Attempt something on a home hi-fi system.

[Station address]   [Your address]

2 July 199X

Dear Mr Owens

I am writing with my demo tape and CV.

I was hoping that you might like to consider using me as a presenter, freelance or staff, for any 'swing' shifts or holiday relief that may need to be covered in the near future.

My availability is as follows: [author's note: try to state days of the week and hours].

I hope you don't mind if I telephone you next week as I would appreciate your reaction to my demo tape.

Kind regards,

Yours sincerely,

Ed Fones

Encs.

Do
Present it on a sensible short duration cassette.

Don't
Present it on a C-60 or C-90 . . . regardless of whether the tape is of chrome or metal quality—it won't impress half as much.

CV CHECKLIST

1. Does your CV scream 'Broadcaster'?

2. List your skills and relevant experience.

3. Express your personality through your CV.

4. Make a professional impression with photographs.

5. Have you bothered to find out the name of the programme controller you are writing to?

6. Type or print your letters on a professionally printed letter-head.

DEMO TAPE CHECKLIST

1. Does your demo show you at your best?

2. Have you included some risqué jokes or comments which might backfire on you? If in doubt—take it out.

3. Is it presented on the correct tape medium; cassette for programme controllers, open-reel for news managers and so on?

4. You haven't put a ten minute demo tape on a silly old C-90 have you?

5. Don't forget to ring the radio station in question to ask for the name of the programme controller, so you can address you package personally. You'll find all the radio stations' numbers in the Radio Authority Pocket Book. Tel: (0171) 430 2724.

6
Working to a Format

WHAT IS A FORMAT?

The way radio stations set themselves apart from other stations is by adopting a format. However subtle or painstakingly obvious it may appear to the listener, every radio station has a format, whether it's a local BBC or a giant independent national station. It is an on-going programming brief which dictates without compromise or deviation the type of service it is offering, ie rock music or news, or overall style and feel of the station's output.

By deciding on a format or station sound, it becomes easier to target a listening audience of a particular age group with similar music and fashion tastes, life styles, eating and socialising habits.

As a broadcaster, it is vital that you fully understand your station's format. It is even more important that you stick to it. If, for example you find yourself working on a 'Gold' all-oldies formatted station, resist at all costs the temptation of slipping in a rock track from the current chart. Not even for a joke or dare because the result is likely to be that you:

● alienate some listeners who will not see the joke, think they are tuned to the wrong station and just tune away
● alienate advertisers who may pull out their advertising campaign
● alienate the programme controller, and you will find yourself making a new demo tape . . .

A word of warning if you are the maverick type. You'll find it near impossible to be naughty or rebellious on the radio without being found out.

Why stations target themselves

Quite apart from being able to offer a unique or different service with their particular style of music or speech content, which is an attraction in itself, commercial stations who depend on their advertising revenue can, with a format, more clearly define their audience. Put simply, they will have no difficulty at all in convincing potential advertisers that the listeners to the station will want to know about their products or services.

Musically speaking—radio formats

For a music station, the easiest way of 'branding' themselves is going to be by the type or feel of music they play. 'Feel' is important because by clever programming a station can create a mood which might be formed by an unlikely combination of artists. For example, it would be very correct for a station with a name like Jazz FM to programme a pop artist such as Sting if a song from his repertoire happened to feature heavily on brassy instruments giving a jazzy feel.

Now you're *talking* radio formats!

Essentially, there are two types of radio station or format: music stations and talk stations. The variations and breakdowns in style are further determined in the type of talk: eg news and phone-ins or news and drama, documentary. And the type of music, eg rock, country, pop or jazz.

A growing radio format is the talk station. Britain's first independent radio station, in 1973, was the 'newstalk' station LBC Radio. Two new 'talk' stations were launched recently: London News Radio (and London Talkback on AM), and the national Talk Radio UK. Together with BBC Radio 4 whose format encompasses news, quizzes, drama and documentaries, and the BBC sports and news station Radio 5-Live, we now have five 'talk' stations in Britain. This is hardly adequate: two or three in every major town would reflect the popularity of the format, and we will see many more in the future.

Is talk radio for you?

If you are the sort of person who loves to keep up with the latest world news events, has a good knowledge of public affairs, and can intelligently explain the latest political or economic crisis, your career should be developed in talk radio.

More choice these days

Have you noticed how the radio dial is becoming a veritable 'high street of choice'? Depending on where you live, of course, the choices of radio station format have blossomed. A few years ago, the radio dial (AM and FM) anywhere in the country was extremely boring. On offer was the familiar Classic hits, local and international news format, all rolled into one. And it never deviated from that format.

Practically every station was churning out the same old chart hits with the same sprinkling of the new. All the broadcasters sounded the same. Even the jingles had an all too familiar sound. And if you happened to have a particular penchant for country music or classical or were a news addict, you had to make do with a few programmes here and there to satisfy your tastes. Specialist or minority interest stations had not yet been given the go-ahead to operate.

All that is changing. It's good news for the listeners and it's great news for you. Especially if you happen to be knowledgeable about a particular type of music, era or have an interest in radio journalism. You might be something of an expert on '60s music—today there are around 25 stations broadcasting an all-oldies or 'Gold' format around Britain.

Take an interest in formats—it's important.

Write, call or fax the Radio Authority for your free copy of: *The Radio Authority Pocket Book*. Updated regularly, it lists all radio stations and formats in Britain.

The Radio Authority, Holbrook House, 14 Great Queen Street, London WC2B 5DG. Tel: (0171) 430 2724; Fax: (0171) 405 7062.

In the meantime a bit of fun . . .

Conduct your own survey paying particular attention to the different music radio formats:

1. Make a '1-10' list of all the stations that you can pick up in your area, including BBC local and national, and local and national commercial stations. Go through both the AM and FM dials from left to right or digitally upwards from 88 Mhz, and make a note of the song or piece of music you heard and its artist.

2. When you have reached the end of the dial look down your list. Ask yourself whether it would be possible to move some of those songs to a different station. Try to imagine how it would affect the rest of that station's output.

3. Would it work? Or would it make the station sound silly? Think about why this is.

4. Think about the types of listeners. Why have they chosen to listen to *that* station? Are they young, or mature, or Asian for example?

5. Are they likely to tune away if they suddenly heard the song that you'd moved from another station?

Fun test
From this list of 15 stations, do you know, or can you work out, the format of each station? All the answers are there in the list, except they have been jumbled up. It's up to you to sort them out.

JFM 100.4 . . .	Oldies? . . .	( )
Country 1035 . . .	Contemporary hits? . . . (	)
London News Radio . . .	Jazz/blues? . . .	( )
Capital FM . . .	Chart hits? . . .	( )
Melody Radio . . .	News/talk? . . .	( )
Virgin 1215 . . .	Country? . . .	( )
Sunrise Radio . . .	Easy-listening? . . .	( )
Classic FM . . .	Dance? . . .	( )
Kiss 100 FM . . .	Asian/ethnic? . . .	( )
Red Rose Gold . . .	Rock & pop? . . .	( )
Piccadilly Key 103 FM . . .	Religious? . . .	( )
Star FM . . .	Oldies? . . .	( )
Magic 828 . . .	Adult contemporary? . . (	)
Scot FM . . .	Classical? . . .	( )
London Christian Radio . . .	Adult contemporary? . . (	)

(Answers and scores on page 147)

SUMMING UP

From your point of view, a radio format is a strict description for the type of entertainment the station is offering its listeners. Think of a format as a sound version of dress code or uniform everybody on the station has to adhere to—a set of rules and regulations that dictates the specific style of music or speech you present.

7
Getting Radio Work in America

PREPARING TO WORK OVERSEAS

Every year, thousands of British people shake their umbrellas dry for the last time, donate their jumpers to the local charity shop and emigrate to countries such as Australia and America.

The idea of making a new life in a far off sunnier land can be very appealing, but it certainly isn't only the weather that helps people to make the momentous decision to leave and start afresh.

More stations . . . greater prospects

Radio in America has a half century head-start on Britain in terms of its spread and development. Add to that America's vast size in comparison with Britain, and a more forward-thinking entre-preneurial business arena, and you have a country which offers a truly incredible scope of opportunities for the ambitious broadcaster, novice or experienced.

Making the most of being a British broadcaster

Tipping the scales unquestionably in your favour is the fact that our American cousins love to listen to our 'wunnerrrful Brrriddish aacc-ent', for many of them a romantic reminder of their own origins.

Good references could add prestige

Those who have worked or have been trained at the BBC will find that it carries a lot of prestige when approaching broadcasting organisations. The two most famous brand names in the world must be Coca-Cola and the BBC.

The World Service has for decades made marvellous work of marketing 'the Britishness of the BBC'. Today it reaches 120,000,000 listeners around the world. Everybody has heard of the BBC and holds its quality of broadcasting and not least its calibre of training in the highest esteem. In fact a great number of overseas broadcasting organisations send their own local personnel, at great expense, to the

BBC in London to be trained in all aspects of broadcasting, reporting and engineering techniques.

THE RADIO SCENE IN AMERICA

An overview of the enormo-US radio market

By the beginning of 1995 there were more than 11,200 fully fledged radio stations broadcasting all manner of entertaining radio in America. Of those, nearly 5,000 were commercial AM stations and over 4,700 were commercial FM stations. The rest are low-key non-commercial operations like college radio and sports events radio. Radio advertising revenue accounts for nearly nine billion dollars or six billion pounds a year, that's 25% of total media advertising spend (compared to a mere 4% in Britain). Radio is big business. The radio dial is literally crammed with signals being broadcast by AM and FM stations. So much so that in some places the signals accidentally overlap, causing reception problems.

The competition is fierce

In some of the larger cities like New York and Chicago, known in radio parlance as 'major markets', there can be more than 50 stations, all competing for listeners. All compete for advertising—as a gimmick, some stations make it possible for advertisers to phone in with a rough idea for a commercial, pass on credit card details, and have the ad read 'live' within a couple of hours. Colourful posters on buses shout the message, 'POWER 106 FM. LA's Hottest Music' or '104 KRBE. Hits Without The Hype.'

Call signs explained

Stations in America are officially obliged by international agreement to use four letters from the alphabet as their station identification or name. To help simplify identification a little, the first of these letters will tell the casual observer which part of the country they are broadcasting in. As a rule, all stations which broadcast in the area west of the Mississippi River are assigned a 'K' as their first letter. Those stations broadcasting east of the Mississippi River will have 'W' as the first letter of their call sign (fig 9 gives examples of the way call-signs are distributed). Although stations are obliged by law to announce their call sign using their assigned letters, some stations make the most of their letters by forming a catchy name. So, KBBX 97.9 became 'THE BOX', WSTR Atlanta is now 'STAR 94' and WMXP Pittsburgh calls itself 'MIX JAMZ 100'.

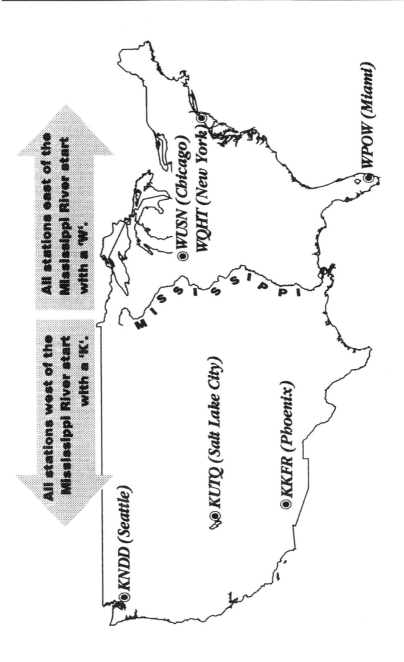

Fig. 9. The 'K's and 'W's of American radio call signs.

American radio formats

Because competition is so fierce, radio stations are formatted in order to make themselves and the services they offer more easily recognisable (see Chapter 6). A station might dedicate its programming exclusively to 'news' or 'talk' or 'hit radio'. They concentrate their programming to appeal to a given segment of the population or given taste in music.

2,650 country music stations alone!

By far the most popular radio format in the mid-1990s is Country, with around 2,650 stations (roughly 1,300 each on AM and FM) rising to meet a resurgence in its popularity. The second most broadcast format in America is Adult Contemporary, not so surprising since this is a demographic area that can easily be commercially targetted— they are working adults. Advertisers love working adults because they have money to buy their products.

AM Stereo

The technology to be able to provide stereo broadcasts on AM has existed for decades. But European radio has yet to capitalise on it. In America, roughly 20% of AM (medium wave) stations have been broadcasting in stereo for a number of years.

They do it standing up

One of the different and perhaps novel ways of the Americans is that they mostly broadcast on their feet. While we British have become accustomed to wheeling ourselves around the studio—the American stands. They hold that this method helps to project the voice properly . . . and dancing around the studio comes very easy this way too.

Some broadcasters sell air-time too

As in Canada, Australia and New Zealand, job responsibilities for broadcasting personnel often overlap. Another very useful string to your bow when applying to American radio stations is being able to double up as a sales person. In a typical working day, an American broadcaster will present his show in the morning and return from lunch to sell air-time on the telephone for the rest of the afternoon.

GETTING A RADIO JOB IN AMERICA

In three easy steps:
1. Register with the Radio Talent agencies.

2. The job offer comes first.

3. The radio station applies for Green Card.

Emigrating to America

Many people have been so intent on emigrating that they have decided to just blindly 'up sticks and go'. Just as many have returned without achieving much except going hungry when the money has run out. Many broadcasters have set their hearts on setting off for the 'united states of radio heaven', only to have their dream shattered by worries concerning visas and the notoriously difficult to attain Green Card, which you need in order to be able to work in America.

You won't necessarily need a Green Card

In America the Green Card is an officially issued permit that allows you to work, either for a few months or sometimes permanently.

Don't panic. Gaining a Green Card is not as difficult as you may have been led to believe. In some cases people don't necessarily need the Green Card. Work visas come in many different forms. You may get an L-1, an H-1 or a permanent visa (these will be explained to you). It all depends on how much a radio station wants to hire you. After they decide that they want to hire you, they must apply to the US Immigration Department for a visa on your behalf. The application will state that you have 'special skills' required for the position they are trying to fill, then a visa is provided. A station might make a case for employing your services rather than those of an American by saying that, '. . . we want to programme a British rock show which needs a British accent. Obviously, we have concluded that no American would be appropriate.'

The suggestions in this chapter form the preferred route for a broadcaster to maximise his/her chances. These are, however, only guidelines and anyone seriously thinking about emigrating to America should read two more books in this series: *How to Emigrate* and *How to Get a Job In America*, which offer detailed information and advice.

The job offer comes first

Today we have a far easier and more professional way of planning properly for a big move like emigrating. Today we have the benefit of 'radio talent agencies'. They work in much the same way as head-hunting agents. For a reasonable fee (around $150–$200) a radio talent (ie broadcaster) agency will work very hard on your behalf to secure a position on a station for you. As soon as a station shows an interest in you, it will take the responsibility for sorting out the legalities like work permits and helping you to relocate. Imagine. It is possible to emigrate to a country like America with a radio job already waiting for you and accommodation already arranged.

Being recognised as a 'radio talent'
In America, broadcasting individuals, agents and stations have no scruples about recognising that every broadcaster is indeed a talented person and promote the craft as such. You will invariably see recruitment ads in trade magazines like *Radio & Records* seeking to appoint, for example, a 'mid-morning air talent'.

See the Useful Contacts section for addresses of radio talent agencies.

DOING BUSINESS WITH AMERICANS

A few tips if you've never had to deal with Americans before and don't know what to expect. Communications can be very fast-paced. Modern forms of communication like faxing and E-mail (electronic mail via computer networks) are in everyday use in America. It is not uncommon practice for a company to ask you to 'fax your CV today' to speed things up. If you are asked to provide your 'T&R', ie tape and resumé, or demo tape and CV—comply quickly otherwise all excitement and interest in you will soon be lost. If you're not very used to sending correspondence by fax, use the services of an instant print shop. It can be expensive, though, when sending a number of them. Generally £1-2 per sheet, but a worthy investment if it's going to net you a golden introduction.

ADAPTING YOUR CV

Your resumé
This is what Americans and Canadians call the CV.

Do's and don'ts
Americans make a habit of *not* including their personal data like their age or ethnic origin (African, Indian extraction etc), or whether they are obese or vertically challenged. They are of the general opinion that this personal information, far from being pertinent anyway, in many cases prejudices your chances.

Discrimination on the grounds of skin colour, age or waist size is not acceptable in America, and every effort has been made in recent years to stamp it out. The things that count the most are: that you can do the job well, and your experience and qualifications.

For a list of major American radio networks, see Chapter 11.

SUMMING UP

Being British, having a good command of spoken English and a good understanding of radio, puts you at a distinct advantage when hunting for radio work overseas.

But don't rush into it. Make as many enquiries as you can before taking off; if possible, arrange things so that there is a job waiting for you the moment you arrive. If you decide to take your chances, getting settled—emotionally, physically and not to mention financially—can be very wearing, and more people give up than succeed. Do contact the radio talent agencies. They have many years of professional experience in dealing with people like you. Their success rate is high, and they are often very proud to be working on behalf of a British broadcaster.

QUICK SELF TEST

1. Roughly how many radio stations are there in the US?

2. What is a 'major market'?

3. What are 'call signs'?

4. What's a Green Card?

5. Do American broadcasters sit or stand during their programmes?

6. What's the name given to the type of broadcaster agency that will help you find a radio job in the US?

7. What do the Americans call the CV?

8
Broadcasting Qualifications and Training

Not everyone can be a broadcaster. But everyone should be given the chance to find out whether they can be a broadcaster.

This book lives by this maxim. But before we take a look at all the educational and training options that are available to you in broadcasting today, let's first try to answer several vital questions—and square up to some important truths.

Do you have ability or capacity?

- *Ability is acquired*: you can have an ability taught to you—the abilities necessary for being a competent broadcaster.
- *Capacity is innate*: generally thought to mean that you can already do it, without any teaching or coaxing, such as a capacity for reading a script at first sight.

BEING QUALIFIED CAN BE A PLUS

Does having qualifications make you an officially qualified broadcaster?

There is no such thing as an officially qualified broadcaster since you do not yet need an official qualification to enter radio, in the way that other industries stipulate required qualifications. You do not need to be qualified to start working as a broadcaster. Companies who recruit externally usually ask for candidates to have a good standard of general education. Highest on their agenda is relevant experience together with a good checkable track-record.

There must be something about you . . .

As with many professions within the creative arts, entertainment and media worlds, no one is going to automatically improve their chances of getting employed simply by claiming a qualification.

Don't forget, we are working in a business that not everybody can easily learn to do. People who work in the arts and entertainment business are there because they are talented or in some way gifted—to varying degrees of course. Each one of us in the entertainment business has a flair or a tremendous enthusiasm for our particular craft. You may be funny or entertaining, artistic and creative, intelligent or good at bringing out these qualities in others, as an interviewer for instance. But you will always have a particular skill or talent.

Can a talent be learned?

Being talented means being extremely good at something. You're born with it, it can't be taught. Just as a woman can be naturally beautiful, charming or feminine, you will be someone who has a naturally beautiful voice or a personality that people quickly warm to.

A talent waiting to be discovered?

Sometimes people can't appreciate their full potential by themselves, and so others help them to realise their gifts.

Some realise their gift at an early age. Most don't know they're good at something until they're quite old. For many, it can take a lifetime to nurture and cultivate their craft. How many painters, writers and composers produced their best work towards the end of their life?

A gift or talent can't be taught. But techniques and correct procedures can be learned. The radio industry is crying out for talent: *your* talent. And it would be more than happy to talk to you and help you to nurture it.

This book therefore assumes that you already possess a skill, a natural aptitude or unbounded ambition, even in small quantities. Something much more than a mere fanciful whim has suggested to you that you might make a good broadcaster, and you want to know how to mould that career.

Will having degrees help me get into radio?

Yes and No. The degree is the finest academic accolade. It should prove to everyone that you have a thorough understanding of a subject area. But it has been argued that a degree can be attained by anybody who has a good memory—not necessarily intelligence. Degrees are very highly regarded and you should be very pleased with yourself. But the degree itself isn't going to get you on the air. Prove to potential employers that you can be a good broadcaster, and then let's talk about how having a degree will help further your career. Your degree is an added bonus, not the ticket that gets you in.

Getting in some radio practice on campus

If you decide to take a degree, a good idea is to choose a university which has its own radio station (see 'Broadcasting on campus radio' in Chapter 4). Many universities have a radio station, run by and for the students, and broadcasting a low power signal to the university campus. Getting involved as a volunteer presenter at this early stage will give you a great insight into radio.

FINDING THE RIGHT COURSE

What courses are available?

There's a course on just about every facet of broadcasting. You may be aware of Media degrees too. If you happen to be taking one already, all well and good. But media degrees tend to cover a range of subjects—one of which might be TV and radio journalism for example.

NVQS, GNVQS AND SVQS

- NVQs. National Vocational Qualifications

- GNVQs: General National Vocational Qualifications (or Vocational 'A' Levels which were taken by 6th form students for the first time in summer 1994)

- SVQs: Scottish Vocational Qualifications

These vocational qualifications are literally work qualifications which certify that you are competent enough to carry out the most vital 'tasks' that would be asked of you in that job. NVQs (GNVQs and SVQs) are based on national standards drawn up by the industry (in this case broadcasting), and they are being constantly updated to keep up with the impact of technological advances. NVQs are not set by outside bodies that may be out of touch with constant changes and developments in that particular work environment. In this way, an NVQ will truly reflect that a person can do the job as it is done by everybody else in that industry today.

Further good news for holders of a GNVQ is that you're more likely to be offered a university place than candidates with 'A' Levels.

Key points about NVQs

These qualifications:

- prove a person can do the job (not whether they have theoretical knowledge)

- identify the standards to be met (as set by the industry, not by trainers)

- can be acquired when needed, in manageable units (rather than whole package courses and qualifications delivered on a 'take it or leave it' basis)

- can be gained in the workplace using flexible learning materials (not off-the-job courses with attendant productivity losses)

- offer a single route of progression from the most junior to professional level (rather than a jungle of qualifications whose relevance to employees' work performance was often in doubt).

They cover most industries and jobs (90% of the workforce so far). And it will soon become the main way of proving your qualification for a job in Britain.

The good news for you is that NVQs are now starting to become available in the broadcasting fields. The first 'pioneering' NVQs and SVQs in our area of work have now been implemented; they are:

- Sound Assistance—Level 2
- Sound Operation—Level 3
- Sound Direction—Level 4
- Production—Level 3
- Production—Level 4
- Production—Level 5
- Production Research—Level 3
- Broadcast Journalism—Level 4
- Editing (to be set)
- Production Operations (to be set)

What the levels mean
- Level 5 = Professional standard
- Level 4 = Higher technician/Management
- Level 3 = Advanced craft/Technician/Supervisor
- Level 2 = Intermediate standard

- Level 1 – Foundation standard

For the contents and structure of an actual NVQ, see page 139.

Research carried out by Skillset has shown that future additional NVQs likely to be implemented by popular demand are going to cover the following areas:

- Digital Audio Techniques
- Financing for Broadcasting
- Interviewing Techniques
- Journalism
- Legal Aspects of Production
- New Audio/Sound Techniques
- Programme Editing
- Radio Editing
- Radio Production
- Radio Reporting
- Script Editing
- Sound Editing
- Sound Editing Equipment
- Sound Processing
- Sound Requirements
- Transmission Technology
- Voice Training

The industry training organisation or 'Lead Body' for all NVQs and SNVQs in broadcasting is SKILLSET, based at Channel 4 TV's headquarters in London. Call, write or fax for more information on the newly available NVQ courses:

SKILLSET c/o Kate O'Connor, S/NVQ Project Director, 124 Horseferry Road, London SW1P 2TX. Tel: (0171) 306 8585/8457; Fax: (0171) 306 8372.

UNIVERSITY COURSES

Most relevant university degrees are formed of a combination of radio and studies in communications, modern or historical culture, TV, film and the press, so it is often difficult to gauge which will be of most benefit to you. You are therefore advised to study carefully what specialisations the degree comprises before committing yourself to three or five years' graft. Some degrees will obviously be formulated with a bias towards electronic media like radio and TV. Others will be geared towards the written word and publishing media, or linguistic, or visual arts like photography and film and so on, with only a limited concentration on radio. Look very carefully before you leap and seek out a degree with a strong emphasis in radio.

These degrees act as a good in-depth introduction to the media in general. Should you at a later stage wish to specialise in one area or another, like a research degree or diploma, the foundation will have been laid. Also, if you have plans to work as a freelance in a variety of areas, a journalist in radio and the press say, a combined degree can be of equal if not more use to you in the future as adequate proof of a thorough knowledge in these other areas too.

WORKING AS YOU LEARN ON-THE-AIR

The following are industry recognised radio apprenticeship training schemes:

London Media
London Media together with CSV (community service volunteers) form what is known as a 'social action broadcasting' group. It's run by broadcasters and radio industry professionals. The organisation is best known for their unique six month radio and journalism course, which offers students the opportunity to join a 'real' radio station and learn how to interview, report, edit and get a grounding in basic broadcasting techniques. For unemployed Londoners (or those who have been living in the capital and have been unemployed for at least six months) the course is free and travel expenses are refunded too. London Media is an accredited centre for the City & Guilds 779 course in media techniques: journalism & radio competences.

Call, write or fax: London Media/CSV (c/o Ben Neild), 237 Pentonville Road, London N1 9NJ. Tel: (0171) 278 6601; Fax: (0171) 278 7912.

The Radio Training Unit
Financed by the GWR radio group, The Radio Training Unit works in partnership with local Training & Enterprise Councils all over the country to provide 26 and 52 week intensive introduction courses with placements at local radio stations. Courses include a good basic grounding in essentials such as: radio studio operation, copywriting, editing, microphone techniques, broadcast law and radio journalism.

WHAT DO PEOPLE SAY ABOUT THE LOCAL RADIO TRAINEE REPORTER SCHEME?

'Getting onto the TRS was easily the most important moment of my professional life. It taught me how to be a journalist—and a broadcaster. A job on the TRS can lead you anywhere . . . it's the opportunity of a lifetime.'

Jonathan Maitland, Reporter, Radio 4 'Today' programme and network TV. TRS 1985

'The TRS taught me to have confidence in myself, it sent me all over the country and it gave me a network of friends who turn up in every newsroom.'

Emily Catto, Radio Journalist, BBC Radio WM (Pebble Mill, Birmingham). TRS 1990

'I spent my first few weeks sitting in a pile of tape wondering why everybody I interviewed ended up speaking backwards! But I soon began to learn the necessary skills and my months as a trainee were among the most productive and exciting of my career. The TRS is the best introduction to broadcast journalism anybody could have.'

Sean Curran, Senior News Producer, BBC Radio Surrey. TRS 1988

'One of the most useful skills the TRS gave me was confidence to cope when disaster strikes—which it often does! The training armed and fortified me to deal with any story—it gave me a great start.'

Charlie Lee-Potter, Reporter, Radio 4 'World at One' and 'World this Weekend.' TRS 1984

'On day one of my second training attachment, I drove 100 miles, interviewed four people and finished after midnight. Three years later, I'm still occasionally doing that—but the rewards? Getting under the skin of an area, following stories through and having network radio and TV ringing ME to ask what's happening at Sellafield.
The TRS is like a good breakfast—it sets you up well for your working life!'

Keven Burden, Westcumbria District Producer, BBC Radio Cumbria. TRS 1989

'TRS—they threw me in at the deep end—but with armbands! It's thorough grounding which has given me the confidence to experiment with the art of reporting.'

Geeta Guru-Murthy, Reporter, BBC Radio Leeds. TRS 1991

Fig. 10. Benefits of the BBC Local Radio Trainee Reporter Scheme.

Full details of courses available locally to you, if you call or write to: The Radio Training Unit, Landau Forte College, Fox Street, Derby. Tel: (01332) 296684.

BBC Local Radio Trainee Reporter Scheme

The number of opportunities for the radio journalist are soon going to be tremendous. The local radio charter for the 1990s says ' . . . and . . . radio journalism must be the grass roots of the BBC's national and international newsgathering operations'.

News coverage on radio is expanding. The BBC has foreseen this and have come up with the Local Radio Trainee Reporter Scheme. The way it works is this: you have a two year contract, spending your first three months on an intensive training course in London. You learn about news, about interviewing and editing. You're taught how to write for radio news, and given an overview of media law—vital for journalists. After that, the training continues with three attachments to 'real' stations around England, and at the end of ten months, you join their 'reporter pool' which serves the BBC local radio chain. You get paid while you train as well: starting salary is around £12,668 plus allowances.

Call, write or fax: BBC Radio Training (c/o Sarah Fuller), Grafton House, 379 Euston Road, London NW1 3AU. Tel: (0171) 765 5303; Fax: (0171) 383 5497.

SUMMING UP

If you decide to take a 'media' degree, make sure that it is concentrated on radio. Not all media degrees are the same.

Remember that there is no such thing as a qualified broadcaster. Qualifications won't guarantee a broadcasting job; they may help. Studying the subject and being trained in the basics may also bring out in you a latent natural talent, and for this reason, training and study is a good option.

To understand the staffing hierarchy of a commercial radio station, see fig 11.

MANAGEMENT

Managing Director/Station Director (BBC and commercial radio)

In the case of a commercial radio station, the MD, as with any other company or commercial concern, is at the head of all financial, policy and decision-makers. S/he keeps a constant check on profits, losses and expenditure of the company. Being also a member of the board of directors, s/he reports weekly or monthly to the board all findings, recommendations for expansion, expenditure or cost-cutting. S/he may be a shareholder in the company, but not necessarily.

In the case of a 'corporation' like the BBC which functions differently to a company and receives the majority of its funding from the Government and TV licence fees, and therefore is not (yet) a commercial company doing business, a title such as Managing Director, Network Radio will answer not to a board of directors but to a board of management.

Station Manager/Station Controller/Chief Executive/ Managing Editor/Programme Editor (BBC local radio and commercial radio)

Station managers and managing editors hold the same office as MD. They are roles that exist mainly in BBC local radio. Since they are not commercial companies and don't have a board of directors, a station manager takes overall responsibility for all departments. Station managers and chief executives also exist in commercial radio, in instances where no member of the board of directors has been appointed to be directly involved with the day-to-day organisation of the station.

Fig. 11. The staff hierarchy of a typical commercial radio station.

Programme Controller/Programme Director/Programme Organiser/Programme Co-Ordinator/Programme Manager/Head of Programming (BBC and commercial radio)

Each one of these titles reflects the same tole. This person is the head of programming and will deal with anything affecting the smooth-running of all on-air output. The main problem-solver and inevitably the person with the most headaches, this person is the final decision-maker with all matters directly related with programming. S/he builds the programme schedule, monitors presentation style and uniformity, introduces programme changes. S/he in effect does all the 'hiring and firing', recruits presenters, arranges fill-ins in case of holiday or sickness. All presenters answer to the programme controller. S/he will also make some final decisions relating to commercial production and traffic. The head of news, reporters and news-readers answer to the programme controller as well as their own section head.

You will discover that on some stations, depending on size and managerial structure, the managing director is also the programme controller: one person taking responsibility for both roles. The programme controller will most likely have previously been a presenter and may still enjoy presenting the occasional programme.

PRESENTATION

Presenter (BBC and commercial radio)

If you become 'someone who presents radio programmes for a living', your profession is broadcaster. Once employed within the personnel structure of a radio station, you are a presenter. A presenter is generally accepted to be someone who presents radio programmes which have a balanced mix of music and speech. A presenter will be able to count interviewing and news-reading among a wide variety of skills.

Talk-show/phone-in host (BBC and commercial radio)

The talk-show or phone-in host is also a presenter, the difference being that s/he has chosen to specialise in a particular brand of programming that is totally speech-based: topical debate and discussion on news and current affairs. The mainstay is phone-ins, where the emphasis of the programme is on listeners airing their views live on the phone and in conversation with the host, who usually plays 'devil's advocate' deliberately in order to elicit heart-felt responses to quirky views. A talk-show may also take the form of interviews with guests talking live in the studio: politicians, authors, psychics etc.

The majority of talk-show hosts are very experienced presenters who might come from a background of presenting mainly music-based programmes, and who have outgrown the youthful excitement of pop radio, preferring to engage in a more absorbing, philosophical and investigative form of broadcasting.

The talk show is the perfect launching pad into radio for someone like a newspaper columnist, TV news reporter/news-reader: a very news-aware person with journalistic *savoir-faire* and enough experience of life to be able to converse intelligently on most subjects.

Travel news presenter (BBC and commercial radio)

The travel news presenter collates and presents live bulletins detailing the traffic flow, bus and train information during the morning and afternoon rush. This type of appointment is sometimes found with individual stations. However, the two key independent companies which supply BBC and commercial radio stations with travel news bulletins are AA Roadwatch, and Metro Networks UK Ltd. (see Useful Contacts).

PRODUCTION

Producer (mostly BBC)

The producer develops a concept or programme idea, sometimes his/her own, and has the responsibility of making sure that the programme is made and/or broadcast to deadline and within budget. Producers might also have to arrange recording sessions and recruit freelances.

Studio manager (BBC radio)

Studio managers work in Network Radio and the World Service on a variety of different programmes, from drama to newsreading. They co-ordinate and oversee all the physical aspects of programme-making.

Production assistant/Programme secretary/Programme assistant (BBC and commercial radio)

The production assistant or PA assists the producer to arrange guest interviews, carry out research, prepare programme materials and time taped segments. Some administration and secretarial backup is also provided by the assistant.

MUSIC DEPARTMENT

Head of music/Music manager (BBC and commercial radio)

The music manager has encyclopaedic knowledge of music and works closely with the producers and presenters. S/he programmes and operates the computerised music scheduling system. S/he is responsible for generating music running orders, maintaining the music database, and is in everyday communication with record companies and music distributors.

Music librarian (BBC and commercial radio)

Librarians work to the head of music, presenters and producers. Responsibilities involve cataloguing and filing new product as it arrives, locating specifically requested singles, albums and soundtracks as they are needed by programmes, ordering new product and arranging prize giveaways.

NEWS AND CURRENT AFFAIRS

News editor (BBC and commercial radio)

The news editor has the final say on which stories will be used (and in what order) in news bulletins. Often this decision is taken only seconds before a news bulletin is due on the air. The news editor will generally have worked as a journalist before becoming the editor.

Journalist/reporter/correspondent (BBC and commercial radio)

The radio journalist or reporter finds and reports stories to the constant pressure of deadlines. This can involve attending public events, carrying out research inside and outside the studio. S/he interviews local and newsworthy people, and sometimes reports live from the scene via telephone or radio car. S/he also edits interviews and creates short report packages for broadcast in the bulletins. On local stations, field reporting is alternated with newsreading shifts on a monthly or weekly rota basis within the pool of journalists.

SPORT

Sports commentator/reporter/presenter (BBC and commercial radio)

This is a radio journalist who specialises in sports comment/or news reporting. Generally, sports journalists are expected to take an interest in all sports; specialisation comes later. Equally prevalent in radio sports journalism are sportsmen and women: retired football, tennis and rugby players who are engaged by radio companies for their expertise.

RESEARCH

Researcher (BBC Radio)

A researcher is an 'information detective'. S/he specialises in collating information (that sometimes involves a lot of painstaking enquiries) on people, events, historical facts, and prepares background information for music, drama, news and documentary programmes. If you're good at finding telephone numbers, names and addresses where others have given up, you'd make an excellent researcher.

TECHNICAL

Broadcasting engineer (BBC and commercial radio)

In the simplest terms, the engineer's chief responsibility is to make sure that the station's signal is broadcast efficiently so that the station can be heard clearly. Any problems thereafter, which relate to anything technical—from changing lightbulbs to replacing faders on a mixing desk, circuitry and rushing out to deal with a transmitter failure on site (at 3am)—is the job of engineers. They also carry out regular maintenance checks on all the electronics, test new equipment, custom design studios and are responsible for the rigging of OBs and stage shows.

COMMERCIAL PRODUCTION

Commercial producer/copy-writer (commercial radio)

This can be a dual role provided by one person, or two separate positions. Commercials have to be costed in terms of studio time, voice-over artist, library music and sound effects. Scripts have to be cleared by the Copy Clearance Secretariat. Music copyright royalties have to be paid. It also involves the physical, creative process of writing the commercials, booking freelance voice-over artists, producing the recording sessions and applying artistic input to the finished product: mixing sound effects and music with spoken dialogue.

Voice-over artist (BBC and commercial radio)

The men and women who work exclusively as voice-over artists are in the main freelance radio presenters and actors, employed by stations and production companies purely on a 'session-to-session' basis to record one or several commercials at a time. BBC radio also employs freelances for documentary and promotional film narration.

SALES, MARKETING AND ADMINISTRATION

Commercial radio generates all its profits entirely from advertising and sponsorship. Sales representatives and telesales executives are recruited to sell air-time. Marketing staff analyse data on audience figures and liaise with advertisers and agencies who buy advertising slots. Advertising campaigns come in many guises; sales and marketing staff will also be involved in formulating on-air competitions and negotiating big prize giveaways with advertisers, such as exotic holidays or a brand new car.

Secretary/clerk/receptionist and administration staff (BBC and commercial radio)

Apart from the people who're directly involved with programmes, there is a large support staff working in radio. Receptionists, secretaries, typists, accounts staff, PR and publicity people, and clerks. They are the backbone of any station as they maintain the smooth co-ordination of all the departments.

Specialist jobs

Non-broadcasting professionals include PR and computing experts. Some broadcasting organisations like the BBC, Classic FM and Jazz FM publish their own books and magazines, so also employ writers, editors, journalists and production staff.

10
The Future's So Bright

The so-called information superhighway is upon us: the coupling of existing technologies such as TV, computer, telephone and cable technologies to form a multi-purpose information, communications and entertainment system. The experts speak of 500 channels of entertainment and educational choice available in every home within a couple of years, and video telephone communication via the TV set.

If radio is to play a part in this exciting social revolution it will have to get itself on the I-Way and be part of it. The first examples of this can already be witnessed as terrestrial radio stations like Virgin 1215 and 1FM are simultaneously available via cable TV and the various audio channels on satellite TV.

GETTING READY FOR DIGITAL RADIO

A recent Radio Authority policy statement envisages '. . . ten to twelve new national stations (BBC and independent); five or six new local stations almost everywhere, with ten or twelve in a few major markets like London and Manchester'.

Broadcasting organisations all over the world were running more tests as this book went to press. The first to start experimenting with high powered digital radio broadcasts was the BBC in London, in 1993. DAB will be phased in gradually alongside the AM and FM frequencies that are operating today. It will take about ten years for it fully to replace traditional radio. This is because the new system operates very differently from the existing one and both the radio stations and listeners will have to get new equipment—the existing tuners and receivers will not be able to receive DAB.

The reason is this: Digital Audio Broadcasting will be a revolutionary new system, a new way of transmitting and receiving radio signals. The difference is that these signals will be broadcast on the higher reaches of the frequency spectrum, in the area of around 230 MHz-300 MHz; much higher than the frequency range used on the present FM wave-band. Because the signals will become digitalised, or compressed, so that each signal transmitted takes up less space on the frequency range, it will leave much more room spare for other stations to broadcast, without the danger of interference.

It means that we will be able to fit in up to six different stations within a space on the frequency range as small as 1.5 MHz.

The trailblazing BBC hopes to launch the first permanent DAB service by autumn 1995. Beginning with regular transmissions in the south of England, it will develop gradually as a national network.

The superior technical capacities of this new technology will offer a much improved sound and reception quality—'CD-quality radio' has been promised. DAB goes into cars too, without any loss of signal in tunnels or when you're on the 'wrong side of the hill'.

Most significantly for someone looking to the work prospects of the near future, Digital Audio Broadcasting will create hundreds of new stations all over Britain which will need to be staffed.

BEING PART OF THE RADIO EXPANSION

Preceding the gradual introduction of digital radio will be another, less radical, technical change to the FM radio frequency spectrum. The Radio Authority is extending the available space on the FM dial that stations are permitted to broadcast in.

Until now, there has been no allocation beyond 105 MHz, on the right hand side of the dial, for any station in Britain to broadcast. This range will be extended to 108 MHz, to allow for 90 new stations to begin their own new brand of radio. It is envisaged that the majority of these will be community stations. No doubt, the more ably run of the stations which have been broadcasting as 'restricted services' or 'festival radio' (see chapter 4), will be given the opportunity to start broadcasting permanently.

SEIZING THE NEW OPPORTUNITIES

We are about to witness an expansion in radio stations, the like of which has never been seen in Britain—and you need to be part of it!

Keeping one step ahead

If you don't want to lose out on the new opportunities, you will have to keep as up-to-date as possible with the latest announcements regarding the appearance of new stations. There are various sources where this news is available many months before individual stations start to advertise their vacancies in the press.

The Radio Authority

The governing body responsible for awarding radio stations with their licence to broadcast is obliged to announce each new award at least six months before that station launches.

Make an effort to contact the Radio Authority every two months to ask them to send you a list of new radio licence awards. This list will contain station names, contacts and addresses. The Radio Authority also produce a yearly 'pocket book' which contains the details and contacts for every commercial radio station which has been licensed by them.

The Association of Independent Radio Companies

The AIRC is the trade association for independent radio companies. It claims to be the 'prime source of up-to-date information about all aspects of independent radio'. New stations join the AIRC as soon as their licence is awarded. Contact the AIRC to ask about new licence awards on a fairly regular basis too.

The Community Radio Association

The CRA is the membership body for community radio. Its primary function is to provide new stations with advice, training and consultancy. The CRA is particularly useful for information on new restricted services. Keep in touch with them regularly. You may also join as an individual member. They produce a quarterly magazine called *airflash*.

Scottish Association of Small-scale Broadcasters

The SASB is the community radio organisation in the Highlands.

The radio and media press

You should also keep a very keen eye on: *Aerial* (in-house BBC magazine, carries many vacancies), *Broadcast*, *The Radio Magazine*, *The Guardian* (Mon and Sat), *The Stage & Television Today*, and *Media Week* for the very latest recruitment ads.

Teletext information

Keep a regular eye on the BBC's Ceefax teletext service for broadcasting jobs advertised regularly.

(All addresses in Useful Contacts.)

BEING MULTI-SKILLED IS AN ADVANTAGE

The majority of the new stations to appear out of the mist of overnight radio expansion will be local and geared toward small communities. They will all be commercial (far from expanding their local radio, the BBC will probably merge existing stations or do away with several altogether).

Smaller stations, covering smaller areas, will attract smaller advertising revenue. This means these smaller stations will not be able to offer such attractive wages as the larger, metropolitan stations. And engaging people who can tackle more than one task would also cut their overheads.

If, as well as claiming to be a competent broadcaster, you could also sell air-time on the telephone, or combine news-reading skills with presenting entertaining programmes, you will make yourself a useful addition to any station's team.

Case study 1—Faye Dir, 22

Faye works for a new community station in Southampton. After two years of operating on and off as a 'restricted service' station in the area, the station was finally awarded the ultimate gift: a licence to broadcast a full service. Faye, who was involved with the station right from the start, also had her patience rewarded with an evening request show. Her work with the station doesn't stop there. She had previously worked with the RAC and knew quite a lot about cars, travel and traffic. At the weekend, she now reports in from the station traffic patrol car, from the town's hot-spots. Her sharp and witty live traffic reports have made her very popular with listeners.

Case study 2—Mick Ser, 27

For three years Mick had been presenting a regular show for his local hospital radio station during his spare time. A successful field sales executive with a computer firm by day, Mick looked forward to little else with so much excitement as to his hospital radio show. It was his passion.

When a new local, commercial station began advertising for presenters, Mick immediately applied. He thought he would try to put to good use his knowledge and experience he gained as a salesman with the computer firm. In his covering letter he stated that although his primary interest was in joining the station as a presenter of programmes, he would also be willing to help get their initial advertising field sales team up and running, in return for the opportunity to develop his new career as a presenter. He is now a

fully-fledged member of the presentation team, presenting the breakfast show, with the additional part-time responsibilities of being the
sales team co-ordinator.

Case study 3—Bernie Simmons, 33 (the author)

'It's Friday lunchtime, 7th October 1994. I'm putting together the
finishing touches to this guide book—the publisher's deadline is only
a few days away. Not only am I excited about the fact that I have
very nearly completed this book but today is a very important day
for the future of London's radio stations. We are expecting the new
Radio Authority licence awards . . . would Capital retain their licence?
What format would the new stations be? Not prepared to wait until
the radio and TV news announced the result, I telephone the Radio
Authority. Capital Radio is to retain both their AM and FM licences,
and the new London licences are Crystal FM, in a 'soft rock' format;
Britain's first God-radio, London Christian Radio AM; the speech
and music magazine-formatted Radio Viva AM; and an FM licence
for Virgin Radio in London. What a week! This news coming only
48 hours after London News and London Talkback first took to the
airwaves. I decide to telephone a contact at Virgin Radio. I con-
gratulate her on the good news, and tell her I am curious to know
what they are going to call their new FM station: was it going to
be 'Virgin London FM?' 'Virgin FM London', or just 'Virgin
105.8 FM?' Nobody is sure, is the answer; and. '. . . in any case, most
of 'em are down the pub celebrating, call back on Monday'. I rush
out for a copy of the *Evening Standard*. I have to know. I switch on
all the radios and TVs in the house, each on a different station and
spend the next hour with one eye on the *Standard*, the other on the
TVs. The ears take three stations each. That's dedication.'

WHAT EQUIPMENT'S IN/WHAT'S OUT?—A FUN TEST

From the list below, which equipment do you think belongs in today's
radio studio, and which is no longer used?

Record turntables	In/Out
LPs	In/Out
Stylus	In/Out
CD carts	In/Out
Tape cart machines	In/Out
Computer monitors	In/Out
Microphones	In/Out

Mixing desks	In/Out
Headphones	In/Out
Reel-to-reel tape machine	In/Out
DAT player.	In/Out

Answers on page 148.

CHECKLIST

1. Have you fully grasped 'digital radio' and it's revolutionary effects on the way radio stations will be broadcasting in the near future?

2. Do you know why the FM radio spectrum will be yielding hundreds of new job openings soon?

3. What efforts do you have to make to make sure of keeping up to date with the latest news and developments on the rising tide of expansion?

4. Why will being multi-skilled put you at a distinct advantage when applying for a radio job these days?

5. After reading case study 3 on page 116, do you conclude that the author might be in need of urgent psychiatric treatment for 'obsessive behavioural syndrome'?

11
Radio Opportunities Around The World

THE ENGLISH-SPEAKING WORLD

The most widely spoken tongue is English. That is, English is 'officially' spoken in more countries than any other language. It is truly the international language.

There are more than 60 countries where English is either the officially spoken language or certainly one of the principal ones:

Gibraltar, Ireland, Malta, Benin, Botswana, Cameroon, Gambia, Ghana, Kenya, Liberia, Mauritius, Namibia, Nigeria, S.Africa, Swaziland, Uganda, Zambia, Zimbabwe, Brunei, Hong Kong, India, Singapore, Sri Lanka, Australia, Cook Islands, Fiji, Hawaii (US state), Marshall Islands, New Zealand, Northern Mariana Islands, Papua New Guinea, Solomon Islands, Tonga, Alaska (US state), Bermuda, Canada, USA, Anguilla, Antigua & Barbuda, Bahamas, Barbados, Belize, Cayman Islands, Dominica, Grenada, Jamaica, Monserrat, Puerto Rico, St Kitts & Nevis, St Lucia, St Vincent & The Grenadines, Trinidad & Tobago, Turks & Caicos Islands, Virgin Islands, Falkland Islands, Guyana.

Here is a list of broadcasting companies and organisations in countries around the world where English is the officially spoken language, or in some cases one of the principal languages.

AMERICA

The following radio networks are the biggest, and own a substantial number of local and regional stations around the country, known as 'affiliates'. Write, fax or call for information on individual stations and regions in their network.

ABC Radio Networks (network president: Robert F Callahan Jnr),

125 West End Avenue, New York, NY 10023, USA. Tel: 001 212
456 7777; Fax: 001 212 456 5397.
CBS Radio Division (network president: Nancy Warren), 51 W. 52nd
Street, New York, NY 10019, USA. Tel: 001 212 975 4321; Fax:
001 212 975 3515.
NBC Radio (network president: William J Battison), 1755 Jeffer-
son Davis Highway, Arlington, VA 22202 USA. Tel: 001 703 685
2000.
Sheridan Broadcasting Network (network president: Jay Williams),
411 Seventh Avenue, Suite 1500, Pittsburgh, PA 15129, USA.
Tel: 001 412 456 4000; Fax: 001 412 456 4040.
National Public Radio (network president: Douglas J Bennet), 2025
M Street NW, Washington, DC 20036. Tel: 001 202 822 2000;
Fax: 001 202 822 2329.

American broadcasting organisations:
National Association of Broadcasters, 1771 N. Street NW, Washington, DC 20036, USA. Tel: 001 202 429 5300; Fax: 001 202 429
5343.
The Federal Communications Commission (FCC) (contact: office of
international communications), 1919 M Street NW, Washington,
DC 20554, USA. Tel: 001 202 632 8400; Fax: 001 202 653 5402.

Highly recommended American radio industry publication:
Radio & Records, 1930 Century Park West, Los Angeles, California
90067, USA. Tel: 001 310 553 4330. (Available by subscription
only to UK customers.)

CANADA

Radio in Canada operates in much the same way as in America; albeit
with a considerably smaller number of stations broadcasting a less
comprehensive variety of formats. Most of the major metropolitan
areas are located very near to the American border, and the American
influence is very evident.

To examine radio work opportunities in Canada, please follow the
same route as for America. Contact the 'radio talent' agencies, given
earlier; these agencies also deal with many Canadian stations in the
same way.

Canadian broadcasting organisations:
Canadian   Broadcasting   Corporation   (regional   broadcasting

operations: Trina McQueen), PO Box 8478, Ottawa, Ontario KiG
3J5, Canada. Tel: 001 613 724 1200; Fax: 001 613 738 6749.
Canadian Association of Broadcast Consultants (secretary: Bob
Lawson), c/o Rogers Broadcasting, 25 Adelaide Street East, 12th
floor, Toronto ON, M5C 1H3, Canada. Tel: 001 613 830 6985.
Canadian Association of Broadcasters (president: Michael McCabe),
350 Sparks Street, PO Box 627, Station B, Ottawa ON, K1P 5S2,
Canada. Tel: 001 613 233 4035; Fax: 001 613 233 6961.
British Columbia Association of Broadcasters (contact: T Peacock),
c/o CKWZ/CKKS-FM, 1275 Burrard Street, Vancouver BC, V6Z
1Z7, Canada. Tel: 001 604 873 2599; Fax: 001 604 873 0877.
Broadcasters Association of Alberta, MG 1200 Radio, #602, 22 Sir
Winston Churchill Avenue, PO Box 1120, St Albert AB, T8N
1B4, Canada.
Ontario/Quebec Association of Broadcasters (contact: K Clingen),
CJSS, 237 Water Street East, Cornwall ON, K6H 1A2, Canada.
Tel: 001 613 932 5180.
Friends of Canadian Broadcasting, 29 Prince Arthur Avenue, Toronto
ON, M5R 1B2, Canada. Tel: 001 416 964 0559; Fax: 001 416 964
9226.
National Campus/Community Radio Association (executive secre-
tary: Jeff Whipple), c/o CFRU-FM, Level 2, University Centre,
University of Guelph, Guelph ON, N1G 2W1, Canada. Tel: 001
506 453 4985; Fax: 001 506 453 4985. (Also produces several
publications on the Canadian radio scene . . . ask to see)

For those with broadcast engineering interests:
Western Association of Broadcast Engineers (president: George
Young), c/o CFCN Radio, Broadcast House, PO Box 7060, Station
E, Calgary AB. T3C 3L9, Canada. Tel: 001 403 220 5769; Fax:
001 403 240 5883.

AUSTRALIA

Ever since 2SB Sydney took to the air with the first radio service,
in November 1923, commercial radio has been alive and well in
Australia. Today, nearly 170 AM and FM commercial stations strive
to keep Australians entertained, city and country dwellers alike.
Future broadcasters should keep an eye on Australia in the next
couple of years, when expansion will open up the job market. The
Australian Broadcasting Authority is right now in the process of
reviewing the broadcasting system, and by 1996 will have determined

what mix of services the listening public in Australia really wants. The broadcasting fraternity is bracing itself for some long awaited good news: the proposal for many more radio services with an emphasis on satisfying the needs of special interest or 'niche' markets.

Australian radio station names

As in America, Australian radio stations also use a call-sign to identity their name. Each station's name starts with a number, to indicate which state it is broadcasting in:

2 = New South Wales
3 = Victoria
4 = Queensland
5 = South Australia
6 = Western Australia
7 = Tasmania
8 = Northern Territory

The letters that follow the number are abbreviations of the company name, city or region the station broadcasts in (see fig 1?)

Important Australian radio industry contacts:
Australian Broadcasting Corporation (Director of radio: PLD Loxton), Ultimore Centre, 700 Harris Street, Ultimo, NSW 2007, Australia. Tel: 00 612 333 1500; Fax: 001 612 333 5305.
Australian Broadcasting Authority, Darling Park, 201 Sussex Street, Sydney 2001, Australia.
Federation of Australian Radio Broadcasters (General manager: J M Rushton), PO Box 299, St Leonards, NSW 2065, Australia. Tel: 00 612 906 5944; Fax: 00 612 906 5128.
Public Broadcasting Association of Australia (Executive director: Ada Hilsoff), Suite One, Level Three, 44-54 Botany Road, Alexandria, NSW 2015, Australia. Tel: 00 612 310 2999; Fax: 00 612 319 4545.

Australian radio industry magazines:
Just 4 the Record (Editor: Brett Van Heekeren), 2MCE Community FM, Panorama Avenue, Bathurst, NSW 2795, Australia. Tel: 00 61 063 33 2790; Fax: 00 61 063 33 2402. (Published bi-monthly.)
Radio Scene (Editor/Publisher: Chris Maitland), Soundplan Broadcasting Services Pty Ltd, Suite 501, Peninsula Business Centre, 20 Bungan Street, Mona Vale, NSW 2103, Australia. Tel: 00 61 02 997 3791; Fax: 00 61 02 979 5392. (Published fortnightly.)

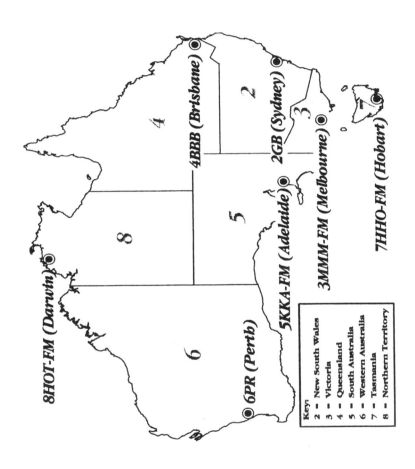

Fig. 12. Examples of Australian radio station call signs.

Australian Film Television & Radio School (contact: Ms Toni Penney), Student Services Manager, PO Box 126, North Ryde, NSW 2113, Australia. Tel: 00 61 02 805 6446; Fax: 00 61 02 887 1030.

NEW ZEALAND

For a surprisingly small number of people—the population of NZ is around 3,350,000—there are more than 140 radio stations. The state-owned Radio New Zealand operates two non-commercial networks, the National and Concert programmes, and 34 commercial stations. The Independent Broadcasters Association runs another 42 commercial stations. A further 16 stations broadcast in the indigenous Maori language. The rest is made up by regional 'repeater' stations.

NZ broadcasting organisations
Radio New Zealand Ltd (General Manager Metro Stations: Ms Lyne Clifton), PO Box 2092, Wellington, New Zealand. Tel: 00 64 4 474 1555; Fax: 00 64 4 474 1440.
Broadcasting Commission, New Zealand On Air, PO Box 9744, Wellington, New Zealand. Tel: 00 64 4 382 9524; Fax: 00 64 4 382 9546.
Broadcasting Standards Authority, PO Box 9213, Wellington, New Zealand. Tel: 00 64 4 382 9508; Fax: 00 64 4 382 9543.

NZ radio news networks
Network News (News editors: Diana Billing and Gyles Beckford), PO Box 3062, Wellington, New Zealand. Tel: 00 64 4 474 1919; Fax: 00 64 4 473 0185.
Independent Radio News (Chief editor: Chris Foley), PO Box 11-757, Wellington, New Zealand. Tel: 00 64 4 473 3535; Fax: 00 64 4 473 6460.

Radio organisations
Independent Broadcasters Association (Executive director: Brent Impey), PO Box 3762, Auckland, New Zealand. Tel: 00 64 9 486 7525; Fax: 00 64 9 486 7443.
NZ Journalists & Graphic Process Union (National Secretary: Tony Wilton), PO Box 6545, Te Aro, New Zealand. Tel: 00 64 4 385 2760; Fax: 00 64 4 385 2902.

HONG KONG

Despite a change in government, from Crown Colony to Chinese rule, it will take an awfully long time to totally erase more than 150 years of Britishness from the Hong Kong way of life. We can assume that opportunities for English-speaking broadcasters will continue to prevail.

The following companies broadcast English-speaking services:
Radio Television Hong Kong (Director of Broadcasting: Miss Man-yee Cheung), Broadcasting House, Broadcast Drive, PO Box 70200, Kowloon Central Post Office, Hong Kong. Tel: 00 852 339 6300; Fax: 00 852 338 0279.
Hong Kong Commercial Broadcasting Co Ltd (General Manager: Winnie Yu), 3 Broadcast Drive, GPO Box 3000, Kowloon, Hong Kong. Tel: 00 852 3 365 111; Fax: 00 852 3 380 021.
Metro Broadcast Corporation Ltd (Managing Director: Craig Quick), Site 11, Basement 1, Whampoa Gardens Hinghom, Kowloon, Hong Kong. Tel: 00 852 364 9333; Fax: 00 852 364 6577. (Runs three networks: Hit Radio, FM Select and Metro Plus)
British Forces Broadcasting Service (BFBS) (General Manager: B Hamilton), BFBS Hong Kong, BFPO1. Tel: 00 852 483 7301; Fax: 00 852 488 5455.

SOUTH AFRICA

Regardless of the recent political change, South Africa will continue to yield broadcasting opportunities for English-speakers.

The following companies run a number of popular and commercial radio stations:
South African Broadcasting Corporation (public services radio: Hardus de Beer), Broadcasting Centre, Auckland Park, Johannesburg 2092/private bag XI, Auckland Park 2006, Republic of South Africa. Tel: 010 27 11 714 9111; Fax: 010 27 11 714 5055.
Transkei Broadcasting Corporation (Managing Director: L Xinwa), PO Box 794, Umtata 5100, Republic of South Africa. Tel: 010 27 471 312 611.
Capital Radio (Transkei) Pty Ltd (Programme Manager: D Smith), PO Box 806, Umtama 5100, Republic of South Africa. Tel: 010 27 471 311 604; Fax: 010 27 471 311 607.
Radio 702 (News-Talk Format) (Operations Manager: R Vickers),

Head office, PO Box 5572, Rivonia 2128, Republic of South Africa. Tel: 010 27 11 884 8400; Fax: 010 27 11 883 1982.

BRITISH FORCES BROADCASTING SERVICE

BFBS, a division of the Services Sound & Vision Corporation, runs a number of English-speaking radio stations located around the world, specifically where they might provide entertainment for British forces stationed there for long periods of time. BFBS have stations in Belize, Brunei, Cyprus, Falkland Islands, Gibraltar and Hong Kong. A significant number of freelances are employed to work on these stations. Contact their head office in London for further details:

British Forces Broadcasting Service (Programme Director: Chris Russell), Bridge House, North Wharf Road, London W2 1LA. Tel: 0171 724 1234; Fax: 0171 706 1582.

ISLE OF MAN

There is one English-speaking radio station entertaining Manx people—Manx Radio. It is given here as it is not governed by the Radio Authority in England.

Manx Radio (Programme Director: George Ferguson), PO Box 1368, Broadcasting House, Douglas Head, Douglas, Isle of Man. Tel: (01624) 661066; Fax: (01624) 661411.

IRELAND

Apart from the state-run RTE, Ireland has some 22 local, commercial FM radio stations which in the main broadcast in English.
For details of how to contact these stations, call, write or fax the Independent Radio & TV Commission (IRTC):

IRTC, Clanwilliam Court, Marine House, Dublin 2, Eire. Tel: 00 353 1 760 966; Fax: 00 353 1 760 948.

Also based in Ireland, with the bulk of its listenership in Britain, is the popular English language pop station:

Atlantic 252 (General Manager: Travis Baxter), Mornington House, Summerhill Road, Trim, County Meath, Eire. Tel: 00 353 46 36655; Fax: 00 353 46 36644.

GIBRALTAR

Three miles long by three quarters of a mile wide, the tiny British Colony of Gibraltar, off the southern coast of Spain, is home to a large community of Britons, and a proudly bi-lingual local community of 30,000 people.

There are two English-language radio stations: A BFBS station (see London head office details, given earlier) dedicated to forces personnel and the British community, and the government run GBC Radio & Television:

Gibraltar Broadcasting Corporation (General Manager: George Valarino), Broadcasting House, 18 South Barrack Road, Gibraltar. Tel: 00 350 79760; Fax: 00 350 78673.

MONACO

A very popular, permanent, 24 hour, English language pop 'resort' radio station staffed by English broadcasters is:

Riviera Radio (Managing Director: Charles Garside), 16 Blvd Princesse Charlotte, 98000 Monaco. Tel 00 33 93 254096; Fax: 00 33 93 304245.

If you're seriously considering working abroad, and you'd like more advice on emigrating and setting up home abroad, you may find it additionally useful to refer to other titles in the *How To* series, at the front of the book.

Glossary

air-time: a radio advertising executive negotiates with advertisers the amount of air-time that is to be paid for, in the form of commercials, promotions or sponsorship.

AM (amplitude modulation): the type of radio signal formerly known as medium wave. AM signals in Britain are mono, although stereo broadcasts are possible, as is the case with many stereo AM stations in America.

back-anno: back-announce. To state on-air what has just been heard; in effect to announce something backwards, '. . . that was Benjamin Creme in conversation with . . .'

BBC: British Broadcasting Corporation.

breakfast show: a fast-moving programme containing lots of weather and traffic reports and news bulletins to get listeners 'wide awake and ready for a new day'. Broadcast at breakfast time, which is generally agreed to be between 6am and 10am, weekdays. Weekend breakfast shows will make less energetic listening, although there is still a need for lots of (shopping, sports) traffic and travel reports. Sunday breakfast, between 9am and 12 noon, is the largest audience-grabber of the week as all the family is at home, creating for the broadcaster a captive audience.

broadcaster: one who speaks regularly on the radio, or presents music programmes, reports, interviews people and reads the news for a living.

cart (a cartridge): a loop tape recording medium, capable of playing a jingle, commercial, sound effect or song instantly. Also fast re-cues itself automatically in preparation for instant play.

cassette: from the French for 'little box'. A compact tape recording medium.

CD (compact disc): the new generation of records. They employ digital technology as opposed to the analogue technology of vinyl records, and therefore offer a near-perfect reproduction of the original. Albums, singles, station jingles, library music and sound effects are played on CD.

commercial: an advertisement on the radio. Can vary in duration from ten seconds to one minute. A cocktail of appealing voice-overs, sound effects and music describes (or exaggerates) the benefits of a product or service.

cue and cue-up: to bring a CD or tape to the desired starting point ready to play.

DAB: digital audio broadcasting.

DAT (digital audio tape): a compact tape recording medium.

dead air: silence. In the case of equipment malfunction or transmitter breakdown resulting in nothing being broadcast at all, an engineer might report, 'we've just had seven minutes of dead air!'

demo tape (demonstration tape): made by a broadcaster or journalist for the purpose of demonstrating on-air abilities. The most effective demos are comprised of snippets of actual broadcasts.

DJ (disc-jockey): one who entertains an audience in a pub or discotheque by playing pop or dance music.

double-header: radio programme co-presented by two people.

drive-time: fast moving programme, similar in style to a breakfast show, aimed at listeners in cars going home from work—generally between 4pm and 7pm.

dry: refers to a recording of speech; an interview, commercial or message that is recorded solus, without any music or sound effects.

edit: taking out unwanted parts of a recording. It is also possible to add to a recording (or edit in); cut the tape, add another piece of tape, and join it all together again.

FM (frequency modulation): the type of radio signal, formerly known as VHF. Once transmitted, good reception of an FM signal is dependent on being in its 'line of sight', thus accounting for reception difficulties in a car, for instance. All FM stations can broadcast in stereo.

format: the word used when offering a definition of a particular station's type of programming. For instance, Red Rose Gold broadcasts in an 'oldies' format.

freelance: one who works 'self-employed', not tied to any long term contract of work.

Gold radio and Gold AM: the type of radio station that offers a format dedicated to 'solid-gold-oldies' programming—music and nostalgia from the 1950s–1980s. In Britain, all Gold stations broadcast on AM. In America 56% of their Gold stations are on AM and 44% on FM.

Green card: American work permit.

ILR: Independent Local Radio.

INR: Independent National Radio.

intro: the musical, instrumental introduction of a song leading up to the start of the vocals. Presenters who want to talk over this will often time it (in seconds) to know when to stop talking.

IRN: Independent Radio News.

jingle: a very short station or programme identification message that is always musical. Jingles are also used in commercials.

jock: diminutive of disc-jockey.

KHz (kilo-hertz): literally, one thousand hertz, or cycles. The hertz is a unit of radio frequency named after the 19th century physicist Heinrich Hertz, who was the first to produce radio waves artificially. You will always see the sign KHz after the frequency location number of an AM station, for example, 1053 KHz AM.

link: announcement, speech or dialogue that is connected to the previous item or introduces the next song, interview or competition.

live: not pre-recorded. The transmission of a programme or coverage of an outside event 'as it happens'.

MHz (mega-hertz): literally, one million hertz, or cycles. It is the unit of radio frequency used by FM stations, for example, 97.3 MHz FM.

NVQ: National vocational qualification.

OB (outside broadcast): a radio programme that is transmitted from an event outside the confines of the studios: such as from the Ideal Home Exhibition, or from a shopping precinct.

on-the-air: the physical act of broadcasting live; being 'on-the-air'.

padding: the art of filling in the spare seconds and minutes when a machine malfunctions or a CD skips, for instance.

PFL (Pre Fade Listening): every mixing desk fader/channel has a button marked PFL. Activating this allows a presenter to balance microphone or song levels (off-air), to prevent distortion or quietness.

phone-in: radio programme given over entirely to listeners' views and comments, spoken on the telephone, live on the programme.

point: forward-promoting a new competition, feature, interview or list of songs to come later in the day, or the following week. A programme controller might ask you to point to (ie talk about) a new programme starting soon.

promo: promotion. In radio, a promo serves the same purpose as a commercial. But in this case promos are short adverts for the station's programmes, competitions or invitation for listeners to write in. Each presenter is asked to record a promo for their own programme. Other presenters then play these promos at their own discretion in their own programmes.

resumé: the name for curriculum vitae in North America.

ROT (Recording of transmission): taped interviews and features are labelled with the date when the recording was made, eg 'ROT: 16/6/95'.

RSL (Restricted service licence): awarded to community radio groups to broadcast experimentally for up to 28 days at a time.

segue: when one song is immediately followed by another, played back-to-back without interruption by presenter or jingles, it is called a segue.

selector: a very popular American programme management computer system used by many British radio stations including BBC 1FM. 'Selector' organises music lists and programme running orders to any given routine or format instructions. The resultant 'selector print-out' is what a presenter works from as a guide to the sequence of songs, format junctions, features and so on.

sound effect/SFX: a pre-recorded noise/sound that is used to enhance or artificially re-create a scene, atmosphere or mood. As a commercials producer, your brief, for example, might be to make a commercial for a football club. You would take recordings of a football being kicked, a crowd roaring 'Goal!' and mix them into the recording to portray an image realistic enough so as to place the listener in the stadium.

splice: the physical act of cutting and joining together recorded tape.

talk show and talk format: a radio programme or permanent station format that is non-musical, purely speech-based.

TBU: telephone balancing unit. The studio telephone switchboard.

voice-over: the spoken narrative of a documentary, commercial or station identification message.

vox-pop: an unrehearsed, on-the-spot interview with a member of the general public. As part of a 'street survey', a journalist asks passers-by for their opinions, and records these for use in a feature or news report.

zoo: an American-imported programme format, usually applied to breakfast shows. A fast-moving programme of 'controlled mayhem'. Both the Capital FM, and the 1FM breakfast shows are presented in this popular zoo format.

Useful Contacts

INDEPENDENT TRAFFIC AND TRAVEL NEWS AGENCIES/SERVICE PROVIDERS

AA Roadwatch, Fanum House, The Broadway, Stanmore, Middlesex HA7 4DS. Tel: (01345) 500600.
Metro Networks UK Ltd. (contact: Will Jackson), 29th floor, Centre Point, 103 New Oxford Street, London WC1A 1AS. Tel: (0171) 312 1300.

INDEPENDENT RADIO NEWS AGENCIES/SERVICE PROVIDERS

Independent Radio News (IRN) (editor: Charles Morrissey), 1 Euston Centre, London NW1 3JG. Tel: (0171) 388 4558; Fax: (0171) 388 4449.
ITN Radio News, 200 Grays Inn Road, London WC1X 8X2. Tel: (0171) 430 4814.
Network News (at Chiltern Radio) (contact: Angus Moorat), Broadcast Centre, Crownhill, Milton Keynes, Bucks MK8 0AB. Tel: (01908) 269111; Fax: (01908) 564893.
Reuters Radio News (at London News/Newstalk Radio) (contact: Nigel Charters), Crown House, 72 Hammersmith Road, London W14 8YE. Tel: (0171) 973 1152.

ASSOCIATIONS, LEAD BODIES, ORGANISATIONS AND UNIONS

The Agents Association Ltd, 54 Keyes House, Dolphin Square, London SW1V 3NA. Tel: (0171) 834 0515; Fax: (0171) 821 0261.
Association of Independent Radio Companies Ltd, Radio House, 46

Westbourne Grove, London W2 5SH. Tel: (0171) 727 2646; Fax:
(0171) 229 0352.
Community Radio Association, *Head office*, 15 Paternoster Row,
Sheffield S1 2BX. Tel: (01142) 795 219; Fax: (01142) 798 976.
— *London office*, Lambeth College, Vauxhall Centre, Belmore Street,
London SW8 2JY. Tel: (0171) 738 8788; Fax: (0171) 720 7518.
National Union of Journalists, Acorn House, 314 Grays Inn Road,
London WC1X 8DP. Tel: (0171) 278 7916; Fax: (0171) 837 8143.
Performing Rights Society Ltd, 29-33 Berners Street, London W1P
4AA. Tel: (0171) 580 5544; Fax: (0171) 631 4138.
The Radio Academy, PO Box 4SZ, 3-6 Langham Place, London W1A
4SZ. Tel: (0171) 323 3837; Fax: (0171) 927 4992.
The Radio Authority, Holbrook House, 14 Great Queen Street,
London WC2B 5DG. Tel: (0171) 430 2724; Fax: (0171) 405 7062.
Scottish Association of Small-scale Broadcasters, 13 Comely Bank
Road, Edinburgh EH4 1EA. Tel: (0131) 332 8270.

THE RADIO PRESS

The Radio Magazine, Crown House, 25 High Street, Rothwell,
Kettering, Northants NN14 6AD. Tel: (01536) 418558; Fax:
(01536) 418539 (Indispensable for news and job vacancies. Weekly.
Subscription only.)
The Broadcasters Q Sheet, The London Fox Publishing Co Ltd, 8
Wickham Avenue, Bexhill, East Sussex TN39 3EN. Tel: (01424)
732 731; Fax: (01424) 733 304 (Useful trivia, historical news,
competitions and programme giveaways for the working broadcaster. Weekly. Subscription only.)

SUPPLIERS OF DEMO MATERIALS AND EQUIPMENT FOR FREELANCES

Canford Audio, UK sales, Crowther Road, Washington, Tyne &
Wear NE38 0BW. Tel: (0191) 415 0205; Fax: (0191) 416 0392.
Studiospares Ltd, 61/63 Rochester Place, Camden Town, London
NW1 NJU. Tel: (0171) 482 1692; Fax: (0171) 485 4168.

DJ AGENCIES

The Clockwork DJ Agency, 25 Sunningdale Close, Stanmore, Middlesex HA7 3QL. Tel: (0181) 954 8899.

DMC Management, PO Box 89, Slough SL1 8NA. Tel: (01628) 667276; Fax: (01628) 669783.

DY-NA-MIX Agency, PO Box 805, Fenny Stratford, Milton Keynes MK2 2TH. Tel: (01908) 270811; Fax: (01908) 270822.

Dings Entertainment (DJ & Roadshows Dept) (contact: Roland Keech), 44/46 Bunyan Road, Kempston, Bedford MK42 8HL. Tel: (01234) 840 800; Fax: (01234) 840 383.

Mervyn Thomas (contact: Mervyn Thomas), 87 Herbert Gardens, London NW10 3BH. Tel: (0181) 965 2991.

Rhythm Rug DJs Agency, 23 Lodge Place, Bristol BS1 5LG. Tel: (01179) 538082; Fax: (01179) 538082.

Universal Booking Agency, 141 Railton Road, Herne Hill, London SE24 0LT. Tel: (0171) 733 3181; Fax: (0171) 737 1777.

Upfront Entertainments & DJs Agency, Andrew House, 60 New Road, Kidderminster, Worcs DY10 1AQ. Tel: (01562) 69433; Fax: (01562) 69136.

Expo Entertainments, Disc Jockeys, 22 Clos des Sables, St Brelade, Jersey, Channel Islands. Tel: (01534) 41649; Fax: Jersey (01534) 41649.

Billy Forrest Entertainments Ltd, DJs & Discotheques, Suite 19, The Whitehouse, 80 Lichfield Road, Sutton Coldfield, West Midlands B74 2SY. Tel: (0121) 354 4258; Fax: (0121) 354 6638.

Leisure Services Agency Ltd (Rank), 439-445 Godstone Road, Whyteleafe, Surrey CR3 0YG. Tel: (01883) 623322; Fax: (01883) 623434.

Midland Entertainment & Management Agency Ltd, Millers Road, Warwick, Warwickshire CV34 5AE. Tel: (01926) 410126; Fax: (01926) 402663.

Mr Gray's Entertainments, 188/192 Station Road, Westcliff on Sea, Essex SS0 7SB. Tel: (01702) 345000; Fax: (01702) 347217.

Northern Linden Associates, DJ Management, Linden House, 24 Norbury Close, Southport, Lancashire PR9 9YW. Tel: (01704) 212364; Fax: (01704) 505197.

Sardi's Enterprises, 6 Redbridge Lane East, Redbridge, Ilford, Essex IG4 5ES. Tel: (0181) 551 6720; Fax: (0181) 551 1200.

CLUBS & DISCOS MAGAZINES

Club Mirror, Quantum Publishing Ltd, 29-31 Lower Coombe Street, Croydon, Surrey CR9 1LX. Tel: (0181) 681 2099; Fax: (0181) 680 8828.

Club Scene, PO Box 11, Bathgate, West Lothian EH48 1RX. Tel: (01506) 54305; Fax: (01506) 630907.

Disco Club & Leisure International, Head Office, 35 High Street, Sandridge, St Albans, Herts AL4 9DD. Tel: (01727) 843 995; Fax: (01727) 84417.

DJ Magazine, Centro House, Mandela Street, London NW1 0DU. Tel: (0171) 387 3848; Fax: (0171) 388 8532.

European Discotheque Review, Waterloo Place, Watson Square, Stockport SK1 3AZ. Tel: (0161) 480 3344; Fax: (0161) 480 8896.

Lighting & Sound International, 7 Highlight House, St Leonards Road, Eastbourne, Sussex BN21 3UH. Tel: (01323) 642639; Fax: (01323) 646905.

Mixmag, PO Box 89, Slough, Berkshire SL1 8NA. Tel: (01628) 667276; Fax: (01628) 668552.

RADIO TALENT AGENCIES

Westwood Personalities (company president: Dick Joseph), 42446 Bob Hope Drive, Suite 228, Rancho Mirage, California 92270, USA. Tel: (001) 619 346 4334; Fax: (001) 619 773 0023.

National Broadcast Talent Co-ordinators (contact: director of registrations), PO Box 20551, Birmingham, Alabama 35216, USA. Tel: (001) 205 822 914.

Jack Taddeo Communications Corp, 20 North Wisner Street, Park Ridge, IL 60068, USA.

Network. Tel: (001) 407 679 8090.

The 'On-Air' Job Top Sheet, 937 Wild Ginger Trail, West Chicago, IL 60185, USA. Tel: (001) 1 800 231 7940 (supplies radio job leads, weekly by subscription).

University and College Courses

COLLEGES OFFERING RELEVANT HNC AND HND COURSES:

London College of Printing & Distributive Trades. Tel: (0171) 735 8484. BTEC HND Business & Finance with a specialism in Journalism.

Cheltenham & Gloucester CHE. Tel: (01242) 532825. BTEC HND Business & Finance with a specialism in Media & Communications.

New College Durham. Tel: (0191) 384 2813. BTEC HND Business & Finance with a specialism in Music Industry Management.

Dumfries & Galloway College. Tel: (01387) 61261. SCOTVEC HNC in Communication.

Falkirk College. Tel: (01324) 624 981. SCOTVEC HNC/HND in Communication.

Telford College. Tel: (0131) 332 2491. SCOTVEC HNC in Media Production & Analysis.

Napier University. Tel: (0131) 444 2266. SCOTVEC HND in Journalism Studies.

City & Guilds of London Institute. Tel: (0171) 278 2468. The course in radio is called: 779 Media Techniques (Press, Journalism & Radio).

UNIVERSITY COURSES

University degrees and diplomas in broadcasting, broadcast journalism and media studies

The following are universities, colleges and institutions around Britain which offer degrees and diplomas in broadcasting.

Anglia University. Tel: (01245) 358 044. BA/BSc (Hons) Combined Communication Studies.

University of Birmingham. Tel: (0121) 414 3344. BA (Hons) Combined Media & Cultural Studies, BSocSc (Hons) Media, Culture & Society.

Bournemouth University. Tel: (01202) 314 144. BA (Hons) Media Production, BA (Hons) Multi Media Journalism, MA Journalism.

University of Brighton. Tel: (01273) 642 815. BA/BA (Hons) Media & Information Studies.

University of Bristol. Tel: (01179) 303 030. BA/BA (Hons) Society & The Media, Postgraduate Diploma Broadcast Journalism

Brunel University. Tel: (01895) 274 000. BSc Communication & Information Studies, MA Communications & Technology

University of Central England in Birmingham. Tel: (0121) 331 5000. BA/BA (Hons) Communication Studies, Postgraduate Diploma Radio Journalism.

University of Central Lancashire. Tel: (01772) 893 896. BA (Hons) Journalism, BA (Hons)/BSc (Hons) Audio Visual Media Studies, BA (Hons)/BSc (Hons) Journalism, BA (Hons)/BSc (Hons) Media Technology, Postgraduate Diploma Radio & Television Journalism.

City University, London. Tel: (0171) 477 8000. BA Journalism, MA Communication Policy Studies, MA International Journalism, Diploma Journalism.

Coventry University. Tel: (01203) 631 313. BA/BA (Hons) Communication Studies, MA/PgD Communication Studies.

De Montfort University. Tel: (01162) 551 551. BA/BA (Hons) Media Studies.

University of East Anglia. Tel: (01603) 56161. BA (Hons) Media Studies with Language.

Falmouth (University) School of Art & Design. Tel: (01326) 211077. BA (Hons) Broadcasting Studies, BA (Hons) Journalism Studies.

University of Glamorgan. Tel: (0800) 716 925. BA (Hons) Communication Studies.

Glasgow University. Tel: (0141) 339 8855. MPhil Mass Communications, MPhil Media & Culture.

Glasgow Caledonian University. Tel: (0141) 331 3000. BA/BA (Hons) Communication & Mass Media.

University of Greenwich. Tel: (0181) 316 8590. BA/BA (Hons) Business & Media Communications, BA/BA (Hons) Media & Communication.

University of Huddersfield. Tel: (01484) 422 288. BA/BA (Hons) Communication Arts.

University of Humberside. Tel: (01482) 440 550. BA (Hons) Communication Processes, BA (Hons) Media Production.

Lancaster University. Tel: (01524) 65201. BA (Hons) Culture & Communication.

University of Leeds. Tel: (01132) 333 999. BA Broadcasting, BA (Hons) Broadcasting Studies, MA Communications Studies, MSc Communications Studies.

Leeds Metropolitan University. Tel: (01132) 832 600. B Eng/B Eng (Hons) Electronics, BEng/ BEng (Hons) Music & Media Technology, BSc/BSc (Hons) Media Technology.

Leicester University. Tel: (01162) 522 294. BA Single & Joint (Hons) Communications & Society, MA Mass Communications.

Liverpool John Moores University. Tel: (0151) 231 2121. BA/BA (Hons) Media & Cultural Studies, BSc/BSc (Hons) Broadcasting Engineering.

University of East London. Tel: (0181) 590 7722. BA/BA (Hons) Media Studies.

Goldsmiths' University of London. Tel: (0181) 692 7171. BA (Hons) Communications, MA Communication, Culture & Society, MA Radio.

London Guildhall University. Tel: (0171) 320 1000. BA/BA (Hons) Communication Studies.

Royal Holloway (University of London). Tel: (01784) 434 455. BA (Hons) Media Arts.

South Bank University, London. Tel: (0171) 277 1091. BSc (Hons) Media & Society.

Loughborough University of Technology. Tel: (01509) 263 171. BSc Communications & Media Studies.

University of Luton. Tel: (01582) 405 252. BA/BA (Hons) Media Studies, BA (Hons) Media Performance.

University of Manchester. Tel: (0161) 275 2000. MEd Education & The Mass Media.

Middlesex University. Tel: (0181) 362 5000. BA Media Arts & Technology.

University of Northumbria at Newcastle. Tel: (0191) 227 4064. BA (Hons) Media Production.

Nottingham Trent University. Tel: (01159) 418 418. BA/BA (Hons) Broadcast Journalism, BA/BA (Hons) Communication Studies.

University of Plymouth. Tel: (01752) 600 600. BA (Hons) Media.

Robert Gordon University. Tel: (01224) 262 000. BA Communication Studies with Modern Languages.

Sheffield Hallam University. Tel: (01142) 720 911. BA (Hons) Journalism, BA (Hons) Media Studies, MA Bi Media Journalism, MA Communication Studies.

Staffordshire University. Tel: (01782) 574 231/34. BA (Hons) Film, Television & Radio Studies.

University of Stirling. Tel: (01786) 473 171. MSc Media Management, Postgraduate Media Management.

University of Strathclyde. Tel: (0141) 553 4170. MLit Journalism Research, MLit Journalism Studies, Postgraduate Diploma Journalism Studies, Postgraduate Diploma Media Culture.

University of Sunderland. Tel: (0191) 515 2000. BA/BA (Hons) Communication Studies, BA/BA (Hons) Media Studies.

University of Sussex. Tel: (01273) 678 416. BA (Hons) English with Media Studies, BA (Hons) Media Studies, MA Media Studies, MPhil Media & Cultural Studies

University of Teeside. Tel: (01642) 218 121. BSc (Hons) Media Technology.

Ulster University. Tel: (01265) 4414. BA (Hons) Media Studies, BA (Hons) Humanities Combined Media Studies, BSc (Hons) Advertising & Marketing (prof. recognition), MA Media Studies, Postgraduate Diploma Media Studies.

University of Wales, College of Cardiff. Tel: (01222) 874 404. BA (Hons) Communication, BA (Hons) Journalism, BA (Hons) Film & Broadcasting, MA Journalism Studies, MSc Econ Media Studies.

University of Westminster. Tel: (0171) 911 5000. BA Film, Television & Radio Studies, BA/BA (Hons) Media Studies.

University of York. Tel: (01904) 430 000. MPhil Communication Studies.

Sample NVQ Structure

SOUND DIRECTION LEVEL 4

This course would be of most benefit to people wishing to specialise in drama production, documentary making and commercial production.

The units—course structure

Unit S21 Direct sound operations to create final sound balance
S21.1 Assess sound sources to optimise simultaneous balance
S21.2 Create final sound balance to production requirements

Unit X6 Contribute to the origination of the creative brief
X6.1 Identify and agree the working parameters of the production
X6.2 Clarify production concept and agree interpretation of creative brief
X6.3 Assess the technical feasibility of the creative brief

Unit S22 Originate and develop initial ideas to meet the creative brief
S22.1 Research and collate information to support the origination of ideas
S22.2 Originate, develop and assess the feasibility of initial design ideas
S22.3 Present initial design ideas

Unit X5 Recommend and coordinate resource requirements for production needs
X5.1 Establish and recommend resource requirements for production needs
X5.2 Negotiate and agree budgets to meet resource requirements
X5.3 Agree and implement schedules to meet production needs
X5.4 Monitor and evaluate the use of resources for production

Unit S23 Assess and select studios and locations
S23.1 Assess studios and locations
S23.2 Agree studios and locations

S21.1 Assess sound sources to optimise simultaneous balance

You will need to show that you fully understand:
What sound is required, and what the artistic, technical and operational requirements are.
Assessment criteria and methods, and how to apply them.
How to identify accurately the characteristics of the sound source.
Relevant acoustic principles and their application in an assessment.
Features and operating characteristics of noise reduction systems.
Compatibility with mono and stereo or multi-channel systems.
Use of format encoders and decoders.
How to identify and contain possible deficiencies in the monitoring system.
Fault finding techniques and procedures.
How to identify/develop and evaluate creative possibilities.
How to explain creative possibilities, options and their implications to people clearly and accurately.
How to deal with others' requests and suggestions courteously.
Who the decision makers are.
How to identify and present alternatives persuasively when needed.
How to negotiate in a way that promotes effective working relationships.

S21.2 Create final sound balance to production requirements

You will need to show that you fully understand:
What sound is required, and what the artistic, technical and operational requirements of the production are.
Criteria for evaluating the sound as it is created.
Relevant acoustic principles and their application in creating the final sound balance.
Compatibility with mono and stereo or multi-channel systems.
Use of format encoders and decoders.
How to identify and contain possible deficiencies in the monitoring system.
How to identify/develop and evaluate new applications of established principles and techniques, and new principles and techniques.
How to explain creative possibilities, options and their implications to people clearly and accurately.

How to assess the artistic and technical worth of the end product.
What the end product is to be used for and possible reproducing equipment.
Ways of identifying and remedying problems in creating the balance.
How to solve problems that minimise disruption to others.
How to explain loss of performance to performers clearly and in a way that is sympathetic to the performer's mood and temperament.
Local documentation requirements.
Cleaning standards, procedures and materials.

X6.1 Identify and agree the working parameters of the production

You will need to show that you fully understand:
What the working parameters are.
Sources of information about the working parameters.
How to assess the scale of production.
How to estimate resource requirements reliably and realistically.
How to budget for the type and scale of production.
Type and availability of equipment and facilities required.
The production environments (studio or location), their significant differences and the implications for resourcing the production.
Recording techniques and processes.
How to contribute to and agree a production schedule.
Nature of contractual obligations and contracting procedures.
Who the decision makers are and how to present information to them constructively.
Who potential members of the preferred team are and how to put the team together.
How to negotiate and agree production parameters in ways that promote effective working relationships.
How to contribute and collaborate with colleagues from different disciplines in ways that promote effective working relationships.

X6.2 Clarify the production concept and agree the interpretation of the creative brief

You will need to show that you fully understand:
How to clarify and confirm client/production expectations.
Types and styles of equipment required in the production.
Recording techniques and processes.
Microphone characteristics.

Laboratory processes and characteristics, post-production processes, sound editing processes.

The effects of special effects processes.

Current and historical arts/media/design styles and their application within the production concept.

How to interpret the creative brief and its technical implications.

How to present, check out and confirm the accuracy of interpretations.

How to present technical information in ways that enable non-technical people to understand its significance for the creative brief.

Criteria for assessing the creative and commercial potential of interpretations.

How to give constructive feedback to other practitioners.

How to contribute to creating the schedule.

Ways of contributing effectively to decision making process.

How to brief others accurately.

Post-production processes.

X6.3 Assess the technical feasibility of the creative brief

You will need to show that you fully understand:

Principles and methods for making valid and fair technical assessments.

Sources of information about the production and what information is available.

How to budget for the type and scale of production.

What safety requirements and constraints apply and their implications for the technical and financial feasibility for the creative brief.

What types of equipment are needed and their availability.

How to contribute to creating a schedule.

What the production values are.

Shooting/recording techniques and processes.

Microphone characteristics.

Laboratory processes and practices, post production processes, sound editing processes.

The effects of special effects processes (aural, visual and physical).

What continuity is required.

How to present assessments, conclusions and recommendations clearly and tactfully.

Post-production processes.

S22.1 Research and collate information to support the origination of ideas

You will need to show that you fully understand:

What sources of information are available and how to access them.

How to use reference material—notes/records/drawings to clarify and assess the parameters of the brief.

Current and historical arts/media/design styles and their application to the productions.

How to keep up to date about the new techniques, materials, fashions and equipment.

How to assess the relevance and value to the production of innovations.

Copyright law, how it applies and how to get copyright permission and licences.

Sources of specialist advice and how to brief specialists.

Requirements and arrangements for storing reference material.

Ways of organising information gathering efficiently and how to maximise information capture.

How to coordinate and agree information gathering activities.

S22.2 Originate, develop and assess the feasibility of initial design ideas

You will need to show that you fully understand:

The artistic, technical and financial requirements and parameters of the creative brief and the production concept.

Precedents for meeting the brief, their features, advantages and disadvantages in meeting the brief.

How to access information about post-production.

Ways of developing new applications of established principles/techniques.

Ways of developing and testing new principles/techniques.

How to develop, evaluate and select options with the greatest potential.

How to present options and clarify the distinctive choices they offer.

What documentation is appropriate.

How to formulate and justify recommendations.

Who decision makers are, and what their preferences are.

S22.3 Present initial design ideas

You will need to show that you fully understand:
Presentation formats, methods and styles, and which combination is likely to have the greatest impact on recipients.
How to use presentation aids and equipment.
What the post-production needs are.
How to select and use appropriate documentation and models.
How to check out and clarify recipients' understanding of the initial ideas and their implications for the production.
How to explain technical issues to non-technical people.
How to justify recommendations.
How to summarise and confirm agreements.

X5.1 Establish and recommend resource requirements to meet production needs

You will need to show that you fully understand:
Source of schedule information.
How to identify specialist requirements.
Alternatives to specialist requirements, and alternative sources of supply.
How to make reliable and accurate estimates and correct calculations of requirements.
What the creative demands of the production are.
How to develop, justify and present estimates, proposals and recommendations.
What presentation formats are required.
What deadlines there are for making recommendations.
Who the decision makers are and how to present recommendations to them persuasively.

X5.2 Negotiate and agree budgets to meet resource requirements

You will need to show that you fully understand:
What presentation styles and formats to use to present information.
What the timescales are for presenting budget proposals.
What to include in terms of reference and agreements.
Sources of advice, including sources for advice about contract law.
General principles of contracting, contract law and how they apply to the agreement.
How to identify and counter objections.

How to handle disagreements positively.

Options and 'fall-back' positions, and how to introduce them into the negotiation effectively.

Methods and formats for summarising, recording and storing agreements.

Commercial confidentiality and how it applies to proposals and agreements.

X5.3 Agree and implement schedules to meet production needs

You will need to show that you fully understand:

What the production requirement is.

Methods for scheduling work efficiently which are appropriate to planning work for the current production.

Application of information technology to scheduling.

Sources of input data about tasks, people, resources, timescales.

Presentation formats required.

How to present schedules clearly.

Criteria and methods for allocating work to optimise matching skills with production needs.

Documentation and briefing methods required to communicate the schedule and the allocation of roles and responsibilities.

Procedure and techniques of briefing people about changes in the schedule.

Reporting systems and procedures.

X5.4 Monitor and evaluate the use of resources for production

You will need to show that you fully understand:

Criteria for scheduling monitoring arrangements.

What best practice in monitoring is and how to implement it in the current production.

Sources of information about progress against budget.

How to interpret financial data.

Reporting arrangements and how to report clearly and within timescales.

Criteria for evaluating resource management.

Types of data needed for evaluation, and how to collate, organise and interpret data accurately and reliably.

Systems and procedures for keeping evaluations up to date.

What the needs of the production are.

How to present suggestions for improvement.

Who the decision makers are, and how to maintain effective relationships with them.

S23.1 Assess studios and locations

You will need to show that you fully understand:
What the requirements for studios/locations are.
Sources of information about studios/locations.
Criteria for evaluating studios/locations.
Assessment methods.
Recording methods.
Quantitative and measurement techniques.
Laws of trespass and how they apply.
Prevailing environmental and working conditions.
Types and availability of equipment, support equipment, costs, timing and scheduling, power requirements.
How to estimate the probability of contingencies.
Health and safety requirements and their implications for the use of the studio/locations.
How to identify costs and construct a budget.
What the demands of the production schedule are.

S23.2 Agree studios and locations

You will need to show that you fully understand:
What the technical, artistic and production requirements are.
Presentation methods, styles and formats and how to select combinations that will have most impact on recipients.
How to assess and present the advantages and disadvantages of sites.
How to check the acceptability of proposals and recommendations.
Who the decision makers are and what approaches are likely to prove most persuasive with them.
Formats and procedures for confirming agreements.
How to conduct agreements in a manner that promotes effective working relationships.

Answers To Tests

Chapter 2 test
You have to commence the sequence by starting the first song at *09:45/52 seconds.*

Chapter 6 test
These are the correct station/format matches:

JFM 100.4 . . .	(Jazz/Blues)
Country 1035 . . .	(Country)
London News Radio . . .	(News-Talk)
Capital FM . . .	(Chart Hits)
Melody Radio . . .	(Easy-Listening)
Virgin 1215 . . .	(Rock & Pop)
Sunrise Radio . . .	(Asian/Ethnic)
Classic FM . . .	(Classical)
Kiss 100 FM . . .	(Dance)
Red Rose Gold . . .	(Oldies)
Piccadilly Key 103 FM . . .	(Contemporary Hits)
Star FM . . .	(Adult Contemporary)
Magic 828 . . .	(Oldies)
Scot FM . . .	(Adult Contemporary)
London Christian Radio . . .	(Religious)

Award yourself a point for each correct format/station match.
More than 13 points: you're practically a pro, what're you doing reading this anyway!
10 to 13: you know your formats.
8 to 10: very good.
5 to 10: not bad.
less than 5: visit your nearest optician.
0: oh dear!

Chapter 10 test

The correct 'INs' and 'OUTs':

I N	*O U T*
CD carts	Record turntables
Tape cart machines	LPs
Computer monitors	Stylus
Microphones	
Mixing desks	
Headphones	
Reel-to-reel tape machine	
DAT player	

Further Reading

UK PUBLISHERS

The BBC And Public Service Broadcasting, Colin MacCabe and Olivia Stewart (Manchester University Press, 1986).

The BBC: 70 Years of Broadcasting, John Cain (British Broadcasting Corporation, 1992).

The History of Broadcasting in the United Kingdom (in four volumes), A Briggs (Oxford University Press).

The BBC: The First Fifty Years, A Briggs (Oxford University Press, 1985).

A Social History of British Broadcasting Volume One 1922–39, P Scannell (Blackwell, 1991).

Let Truth Be Told, G Mansell (Weidenfeld and Nicolson, 1982).

A Skyful of Freedom, A Walker (Broadside Books, 1992).

Into The Wind, J C W Reith (Hodder and Stoughton, 1949)

D G: The Memoirs of a British Broadcaster, A Milne (Hodder, 1988).

British Broadcasting, A Smith (ed) (David and Charles, 1974).

The Most Contrary Region, The BBC in Northern Ireland 1924–84, R Cathcart (Blackstaff Press, 1984).

BBC Engineering 1922–72, E Pawley (British Broadcasting Corporation, 1972).

Who's Listening? The Story of BBC Audience Research, R Silvey (Allen and Unwin, 1977).

Learning Over The Air: 60 Years of Partnership in Adult Education, J Robinson (British Broadcasting Corporation, 1982).

The Radio Companion, P Donovan (Harper Collins, 1991).

Early Wireless, A Constable (Midas, 1980).

Laughter in the Air: An Informal History of British Radio Comedy, B Took (Robson, 1981).

Broadcasting in the UK: A Guide to Information Sources, B MacDonald (Mansell, 1988).

US PUBLISHERS

A Pictorial History of Radio, Irving Settel (Grossett and Dunlap, 1967).

The Big Broadcast, 1920–1950, Frank Buxton and Bill Owen (Viking, 1972).

Don't Touch That Dial: Radio Programming in American Life, 1920–1960, J Fred McDonald (Nelson Hall, 1979).

Connections: Reflections on Sixty Years of Broadcasting, Mary C O'Connell (National Broadcast Company, 1986).

Radio's Golden Years: The Encyclopaedia of Radio Programmes, 1930–1960, Vincent Terrace (A S Barnes and Co, 1981).

The DJs, Arnold Passman (Macmillan, 1971).

Talk Radio and the American Dream, Murray B Levin (Lexington Books, 1987).

Broadcasting/Cable Yearbook (Broadcasting Publications, annual).

Making It in Radio: Your Future in the Modern Medium, Dan Blum (Continental Media Company, 1983).

Breaking in Broadcasting: Getting a Good Job in Radio or TV Out Front or Behind the Scenes, Donn Pearlman (Bonus Books, 1986).

Exploring Careers in Broadcast Journalism, Rod Vahl (Richards Rosen Press, 1983).

How to Break Into the Media Professions, A Zimmerman (Doubleday, 1981).

Radio's 100 Men of Science, Orrin E Dunlap Jr (Harper and Brothers 1944).

Fundamentals of Radio Broadcasting, John Hasling (McGraw-Hill, 1980).

Radio Research, Paul F Lazarfield and Frank N Stanton (Dyell, Sloan and Pearce, 1942).

My Father Marconi, Degna Marconi (McGraw-Hill, 1962).

News On The Air, Paul White (Harcourt Brace, 1947).

AUSTRALIAN PUBLISHERS

History and Development of the ABC (Australian Broadcasting Corporation, 1983).

Commercial Media in Australia: Economics, Ownership, Technology and Regulation, Alan G Brown (University of Queensland Press, 1986).

Index

How to Write for Television
William Smethurst

Television is a huge and expanding market for the freelance writer. Particularly in the field of drama, producers are constantly looking for new writers for situation comedies, series drama, and soap operas and single plays. But what kind of scripts are required? How should a script be presented and laid out? What camera moves should you put in, and should you plan for commercial breaks? Which programmes and organisations should you contact, and which are the subjects to tackle or avoid? Packed with hard-hitting information and advice, and illustrated throughout with examples, this is a complete step-by-step manual for every writer wanting to break into this lucrative market. 'Packed with information which is well presented and easily accessible.' *National Association of Careers & Guidance Teachers Bulletin.* 'If would be TV scriptwriters are looking for a wide ranging and practical book to light the fuse which could lead to a successful career, they should certainly invest in a copy of William Smethurst's *How to Write for Television.*' *BAFTA News.* 'Your best starting point is probably William Smethurst's book.' *Writers News.* William Smethurst has written numerous scripts for both radio and television. He has been a television script editor at BBC Pebble Mill, and executive producer of drama serials for Central Television. He is now a director of the Independent television company, Andromeda Television Ltd.

160pp illus. 1 85703 045 1.

How to Live & Work in Germany
Christine Hall

Whether you are planning to relocate for three months or three years, this is the book for you. Completely rewritten to reflect the latest developments, this latest edition covers such practical topics as entry requirements, transportation, money matters, housing, schools, insurance and much besides. It also includes valuable pointers to German values, customs, business practices and etiquette to help you make the most of your stay. 'Detailed help is given on how to find work in Germany including . . . a comprehensive list of organisations which offer the chance to combine the experience of living in Germany with a useful activity.' *Phoenix/Association of Graduate Careers Advisory Services.*

142pp illus. 1 85703 125 3. Second edition.

How to Get into Films and TV
Robert Angell
Foreword by David Puttnam

Would you like to make a career in films or television? Whether you want to direct feature films, photograph documentaries, edit commercials or pop videos, write current affairs programmes for television, do artwork for animation or just know that you want to be involved in film or television in some capacity but are not quite sure how to set about getting started, this book will give you a wealth of information to guide you through the dense but exotic jungle of these exciting industries. Previous edition published as **How to Make it in Films & TV.** 'Readable and useful . . . At the back of the book is a useful section on writing letters/phoning/mailshots, and appendix and glossary.' *Amateur Film and Video Maker.* 'An indepth coverage of the subject. Offers a wealth of useful advice and addresses for more information . . . One of the essential references for careers libraries.' *The Careers Officer Journal.* 'A comprehensive guide in lay language . . . Each section includes suggested starting points for newcomers.' *BAFTA News.* 'Want to break into films and TV? Don't know how to go about it? Then look no further, for you'll find all the answers to your questions in Robert Angell's *How to Make It in Films & TV.* In it you'll find the various ways and means of getting into the industry, along with explanations of the various jobs available, and how they fit into the general pattern of film and programme-making.' *Film Review.* Robert Angell is a Council Member of the British Academy of Film & Television Arts (BAFTA) and Chairman of its Programme Committee and Short Film Award jury.

144pp illus. 1 85703 162 8. Third edition.

How to Write for Publication
Chriss McCallum

'How can I sell my work? How do I protect my copyright? Can a magazine steal my story? Why just a printed rejection slip—can't editors tell me where I'm going wrong? Are writing courses worth the money? Should I get an agent?' Highly expert and practical, **How to Write for Publication** gives the often surprising answers to these and hundreds of other questions most often asked by the great silent majority of struggling writers, whether of fiction, nonfiction, poetry, drama, stories or articles. No author seriously interested in getting published can afford to be without this manual, packed with checklists, examples and key contacts. 'Handy for both professional and newcomer alike.' *Writers News*. 'Everything you ever wanted to know about the practical side of publishing . . . excellent.' *Competitors Journal*. 'Really definitive . . . Leaves every other similar book in the shade.' *Pause (National Poetry Foundation)*. 'It is, quite simply, one of the best books of its kind that I've ever read.' Steve Wetton, author of BBC TV's comedy drama *Growing Pains*. 'The revised edition maintains the high standard . . . Its reference section of useful addresses is value for money on its own.' *Writers News*. Chriss McCallum has many years' experience as a professional Editor, and has worked for Collins, Penguin, W H Allen and other leading firms. She was a publisher of *The Writers Voice* (1983–86) and is a Member of the Society of Authors, The Society of Women Writers & Journalists, and an Honorary Member of the Comedy Writers Association.

192pp illus. 1 85703 140 7. Third edition.

How to Get That Job
Joan Fletcher

Now in its third edition this popular book provides a clear step-by-step guide to identifying job opportunities, writing successful application letters, preparing for interviews and being selected. 'A valuable book.' *Teachers Weekly*. 'Cheerful and appropriate . . . particularly helpful in providing checklists designed to bring system to searching for a job. This relaxed, friendly and very helpful little book could bring lasting benefit.' *Times Educational Supplement*. 'Clear and concise . . . should be mandatory reading by all trainees.' *Comlon Magazine (LCCI)*. Joan Fletcher is an experienced Manager and Student Counsellor.

112pp illus. 1 85703 096 6. Third edition.

How to Do Your Own Advertising
Michael Bennie

'Entrepreneurs and small businesses are flooding the market with new products and services; the only way to beat the competition is successful selling—and that means advertising.' But what can you afford? This book is for anyone who needs—or wants—to advertise effectively, but does not want to pay agency rates. Michael Bennie is Director of Studies at the Copywriting School. 'An absolute must for everyone running their own small business . . . Essential reading . . . Here at last is a practical accessible handbook which will make sure your product or service gets the publicity it deserves.' *Great Ideas Newsletter (Business Innovations Research)*. 'Explains how to put together a simple yet successful advertisement or brochure with the minimum of outside help . . . amply filled with examples and case studies.' *First Voice (National Federation of Self Employed and Small Businesses)*.

176pp illus. 0 7463 0579 6.

How to Find Temporary Work Abroad
Nick Vandome

Would you like the chance to work abroad—perhaps to expand your horizons, finance an extended holiday, or use some 'time between'? Whatever your aims and interests, this practical book has something for you. It explains where to find the opportunities suited to your own particular interests, how to apply and be selected, how to manage money, passports, permits, insurance and accommodation, and how to get the most out of your experience overseas. Whether you plan to stay abroad for a couple of weeks or most of the year, this is the book for you, packed with valuable employment advice and contacts. Nick Vandome is a young freelance writer who has spent a year abroad on three occasions, in France, Australia, Africa and Asia. His articles have appeared in *The Guardian, The Scotsman, The Daily Telegraph* and elsewhere. He is also author of *How to Get a Job in Australia* in this series.

160pp illus. 1 85703 109 1.

How to Get a Job in America
Roger Jones

Updated and revised, this book helps you to turn your dream into reality by explaining the work possibilities open to non-US citizens. Drawing on the experience of individuals, companies and recruitment agencies Roger Jones reveals the range of jobs available, the locations, pay and conditions, and how to get hired. This is an essential handbook for everyone planning to work in the US, whether on a short-term vacation assignment, on secondment or contract, or on a permanent basis. Roger Jones is a freelance author specialising in careers and expatriate matters and has himself worked overseas. 'Essential for anyone who is thinking of working in the US.' *Going USA.* 'Outlines with some thoroughness the procedures a future immigrant or temporary resident would have to undertake . . . For young people considering a US exchange or summer employment the section on vacation jobs is particularly worthwhile.' *Newscheck/ Careers Service Bulletin.* 'Very good value for money.' *School Librarian journal.*

224pp illus. 1 85703 168 7. Third edition.

How to Live & Work in America
Steve Mills

Now in its third edition this highly readable and informative handbook explains America's rules and regulations on immigration: a jungle of quotas, green cards and special categories, plus work and lifestyle prospects in this ultimate land of opportunity. 'The scope and presentation of the material is excellent, well worth buying.' *Nexus Expatriate Magazine.* 'Very useful and informative . . . It contains much information about the rules and regulations on immigration, normally difficult to obtain from official sources . . . A mine of information and a must for potential US visitors.' *The Expatriate.* 'An entertaining anecdotal and diverse book.' *Newscheck/ Careers Service Bulletin* 'A must . . . Has all the information that you could want.' *Going USA.* Steve Mills lectures at the David Bruce Centre for American Studies at the University of Keele and has himself spent five years living and working in the USA.

222pp illus. 1 85703 136 9. Third edition.

How to Get a Job Abroad
Roger Jones

Now in a third fully revised edition, this top-selling title is essential for everyone planning to spend a period abroad. It contains a big reference section of medium and long-term job opportunities and possibilities, arranged by region and country of the world, and by profession/occupation. There are more than 100 pages of specific contacts and leads, giving literally hundreds of updated addresses and much hard-to-find information. There is a classified guide to overseas recruitment agencies, and even a multi-lingual guide to writing application letters. 'A fine book for anyone considering even a temporary overseas job.' *The Evening Star.* 'A highly informative and well researched book . . . containing lots of hard information and a first class reference section . . . A superb buy.' *The Escape Committee Newsletter.* 'A valuable addition to any careers library.' *Phoenix (Association of Graduate Careers Advisory Services).* 'An excellent addition to any careers library . . . Compact and realistic . . . There is a wide range of reference addresses covering employment agencies, specialist newspapers, a comprehensive booklist and helpful addresses . . . All readers, whether careers officers, young adults or more mature adults, will find use for this book.' *Newscheck/Careers Services Bulletin.* Roger Jones has himself worked abroad for many years and is a specialist writer on expatriate and employment matters.

272pp illus. 1 85703 115 6. Third edition.

How to Market Yourself
Ian Phillipson

In today's intensely competitive workplace it has become ever more vital to market yourself effectively, whether as a first-time job hunter, existing employee, or mature returner. This hard-hitting new manual provides a really positive step-by-step guide to assessing yourself, choosing the right personal image, identifying and presenting the right skills, building confidence, marketing yourself in person and on paper, organising your self-marketing campaign, using mentors at work, selling yourself to colleagues, clients and customers, and marketing yourself for a fast-changing future. The book is complete with checklists, assignments and case studies.

160pp illus. 1 85703 160 1.